Point
Click &
Wow!

Point Click & Wow!

A Quick Guide to Brilliant Laptop Presentations

SECOND EDITION

Claudyne Wilder
Jennifer Rotondo

JOSSEY-BASS/PFEIFFER
A Wiley Company
www.pfeiffer.com

JOSSEY-BASS/PFEIFFER

A Wiley Company
989 Market Street
San Francisco, CA 94103-1741
415.433.1740; Fax 415.433.0499
800.274.4434; Fax 800.569.0443

www.pfeiffer.com

Jossey-Bass/Pfeiffer is a registered trademark of Jossey-Bass Inc., A Wiley Company.

ISBN: 0-7879-5669-4

Library of Congress Cataloging-in-Publication Data
Wilder, Claudyne.
  Point, click & wow! : a quick guide to brilliant laptop
presentations / Claudyne Wilder, Jennifer Rotondo.—2nd ed.
     p. cm.
Includes index.
  ISBN 0-7879-5669-4 (alk. paper)—ISBN 0-9990000-5-5 (CD-ROM)
  1. Business presentations—Graphic methods. 2. Multimedia
systems in business presentations. I. Title: Point, click, and
wow. II. Rotondo, Jennifer. III. Title.
  HF5718.22 .W55 2001
  658.4'5—dc21   2001005073

Printed in the United States of America

Credits are on p. 228

We at Jossey-Bass strive to use the most environmentally sensitive paper stocks available to us. Our publications are printed on acid-free recycled stock whenever possible, and our paper always meets or exceeds minimum GPO and EPA requirements.

Acquiring Editor: Josh Blatter
Director of Development: Kathleen Dolan Davies
Editor: Rebecca Taff
Production Editor: Dawn Walker
Manufacturing Supervisor: Becky Carreño
Interior Design: Gene Crofts
Cover Design: Bruce Lunquist
Illustrations: Bruce Cormack

Printing 10   9   8   7   6   5   4   3   2   1

To my husband Tad, who dances with me through life.

To my husband Mike, for completing me.
To my four remarkable children, who enlighten me daily.
To my Lord, for blessing me with the knowledge that I share with you.
To Claudyne, for putting up with me and my busy schedule.

Contents

3   Prepare for Technology Success   59

4   Design Corporate Blueprints   95

Acknowledgments

We would first like to thank all our clients, the participants in our seminars, and those of you whom we only know through e-mail. Claudyne thanks her husband, Tad Jankowski, who encouraged her to work smarter, not more, so they could go out and play. Claudyne also thanks all clients and the participants in her Winning Presentation seminars and Creating High-Impact Visual seminars who taught her about the delights and perils of computer-generated presentations. She thanks the more than one hundred people on her e-newsletter mailing list who responded to her questions about laptop presentations and appreciates their willingness to share insights, frustrations, and desires so that others can create and give more effective presentations.

Jennifer thanks her staff of designers and project managers, who help keep her presentation design company, Creative Minds, Inc., thriving. She sends a special thanks to her many clients, students, and followers, who allow her to express her unique creative flair through her design, writing, and teaching.

We are pleased to thank the following individuals and companies in particular for making this book possible: Pam Campagna, Gary Kayye, Mimi Ohlinger, Roger Parker, Ellen Finkelstein, and Renate Rooney, who read specific chapters and offered their expert advice. We also thank the following companies and people who graciously shared their ideas and/or slides with us: CMD Group, Marlene Dunham at The College Board, deliveretoday, EMS, Harmon, Inc., IIAA, Intellivoice, Greg Rocco at Mercury Computer, Paquita Bath and Carol DuPre at The Nature Conservancy, John Akins at S&K, and Fletcher Birmingham at Summit Business-Consulting, Inc., the employees at Transchannel, Towne Services, Inc., Eugene Degenhardt at the U.S. Army Corps of Engineers, Priscilla Fraser, Melissa Rodgers, Renee Atkinson, and Heather Stefl. We thank Tad Simons and Julie Hill at *Presentations* Magazine, who have supported our Before and After Column, which has given us many opportunities to discuss presentations with people around the world. We thank the people at Crystal Graphics, who supplied a demo of their products for the book's CD.

We also thank Kathleen Dolan Davies and Dawn Walker at Jossey-Bass, who kept moving the project along. Dawn was especially good at organizing all the files for the book and the CD. Plus, we thank our editor Rebecca Taff, who helped to craft the final phrases and organization of the book.

Foreword

Roger C. Parker

Good news! Never again will you be alone in front of a room where you have to give a presentation. By your side, acting as your personal coaches and mentors, are Claudyne Wilder, coauthor of the first edition of *Point, Click & Wow!* and Jennifer Rotondo, coauthor of the CD: *Slides That Win: Your Roadmap to Success.*

The first edition of this book has long been one of my favorites, and I've long respected Claudyne's design abilities. In fact, there are magazines that I subscribe to simply to read her and Jennifer's monthly columns on presentation design and technique. Enhancing the accumulated wisdom of Claudyne Wilder and the more than one hundred presenters who have contributed their accumulated wisdom are the graphic designs of Jennifer Rotondo. Jennifer's ability to translate words and numbers into compelling, memorable graphics adds an all-important element to this book.

Through Jennifer's examples, you'll learn the right and wrong ways to use color, text, and backgrounds, as well as when (and when not) to use advanced effects such as animations, transfers, and builds. You'll also learn how to use your presentation visuals to reinforce, not undermine, your firm's (or client's) corporate image.

In the revised edition of this classic book, Claudyne and Jennifer expand on the ideas expressed in the first edition and include numerous tips on using the latest technology effectively.

But there's more. They aren't the only ones by your side. More than one hundred experienced presenters from around the world have contributed tips and techniques they've learned the hard way. Their first-hand stories give this book a real-world orientation unavailable from any other book.

You'll learn the right and wrong things to do when creating and delivering your next presentation. You'll see how the tiniest details can contribute to, or derail, your presentation. You'll find out what to do and what not to do while preparing and delivering your presentation.

As you read this book, you'll find that the process of creating and delivering presentations doesn't have to be a stressful experience. By incorporating the ideas in this book, you'll soon look forward to developing and fine-tuning your own laptop presentations.

There are lots of books about presentation theory, lots of books about presentation software, and lots of books about designing good-looking presentation visuals. But *Point, Click & Wow!* has always occupied a special place in my bookcase because it was the only book that smoothly covered all the bases, from planning your message through design, delivery, and on-the-spot problem solving using your laptop.

Point, Click & Wow! teaches by example. No theory here; just hundreds of tips and techniques that, taken together, can build the confidence of even the most nervous presenter. You'll not only learn what to do, but more important, how to plan ahead so you'll be prepared for the inevitable snafus that plague even the most experienced presenter. You'll feel your confidence building as you realize that most presentation problems can be anticipated and solved ahead of time. By preparing for the worst possible scenarios, you can come out looking like a hero.

Point, Click & Wow! is a working document. It's a guide to keep by your computer where you can easily refer to it as you prepare your presentations.

Each chapter contains numerous examples that bring the text to life and concludes with a checklist to help you make sure that your presentation content, design, and delivery are focused on the task at hand and that you haven't inadvertently left anything out. Photocopy the checklists in each chapter and distribute copies to your co-workers so that, together, you can keep your presentations as on-target as possible.

Let *Point, Click & Wow!* be your guide to smooth, stress-free, and trouble-free laptop presentations that build your confidence and achieve the desired results. Put *Point, Click & Wow!* to work, and be prepared for the applause and praise that's sure to follow at the conclusion of your upcoming presentations for years to come.

Roger C. Parker
Dover, NH
May 2001
www.NewEntrepreneur.com

Introduction

Point, Click & Wow! A Quick Guide to Brilliant Laptop Presentations. Many people would read this title and think it's all about making the most dazzling slides possible. "Just wow the audience with the slides," they would suggest, meaning that you don't have to do anything else but show animated, razzle-dazzle slides. The audience will then go along with your recommendations. However, this is just not true.

Today more and more businesses are using electronic equipment to make presentations, yet those given the task aren't always sure what to do or how to do it. Unfortunately, people end up learning from their failures or the failures of those they watch giving presentations. As companies make greater and greater capital investments in presentation technology, employees often end up struggling to use it effectively.

A "Wow!" from your audience comes after the presentation. It comes by your having interacted with them and convinced them that they count. They become so engaged that when they leave the room they say things like, "I really learned useful information from the talk. The discussions in the room were helpful to my work."

This may sound contradictory, but today to give a brilliant laptop presentation you almost don't give it. You must interact with your audience, and they must interact with you. This book takes you through the steps for creating more dialogues and discussions with your audience and fewer monologues.

We wrote this book to enable all businesspeople, salespeople included, to use this new technology creatively and effectively and to communicate better. Our basic premise is that technology is fantastic, but it will never take the place of a well-prepared, enthusiastic, audience-oriented presenter. This book is intended for people who present with a computer, whether it is a laptop or some other type of computer equipment.

Overview of the Book

Chapter 1, Connect to Your Audience, encourages you to consider how you can engage the audience. Too many people are standing in front of audiences and just talking through their slides. Sometimes they don't even ask enough questions to find out who is sitting in the audience and for what purpose. This chapter explains how to craft your presentation for audience involvement in order to create a two-way informational exchange.

Presenters often forget this point: *You are the message.* The computer is only a tool; your audience is there to see and hear your personality, your enthusiasm, and your ability to respond to their questions and concerns extemporaneously. People must buy *you,* as well as your fancy presentation. Effective communication skills are one of the most important requirements for success.

Chapter 2, Organize Focused on One Objective, encourages you not to create a single slide until you have seriously considered and discussed your presentation's objective with others. As presenters find it increasingly easy to create slides, they leave out one of the most important elements—creating a focused, coherent presentation. The Presentation Overview Checklist we provide gives you a way to organize your talk before you begin creating or pulling together slides. The Presentation Overview Checklist is also on the CD for ease of use. You'll also see some suggested formats for organizing.

Chapter 3, Prepare for Technology Success, provides some real-world examples of what can happen when people do or do not prepare for giving laptop presentations. When you have some ideas of what can go wrong, you are more likely to prepare ahead of time. Then you can relax during the talk, as you'll have a backup plan place. When you are comfortable using the new technology, you will come across as a personable, sincere presenter.

For those of you new to using technology, we plan to make your initial entry a success. For those of you already involved, we plan to add to your reservoir of knowledge, thus preventing you from experiencing certain technology problems. Even if you have access to an expert at all times, you still need to learn some basic skills, and you need to know the key questions to ask your technical people and the audiovisual staff at hotels and conference centers where you present.

Chapters 4 and 5 provide some specific ideas on how to save hours of time when creating slides for a laptop presentation. For example, you will create your slides differently if you are using a remote mouse, so you must think about your technology capabilities before you create any slides.

Chapter 4, Design Corporate Blueprints, speaks to those hundreds of thousands of people who spend hours attempting to create effective slides. We suggest that companies become smarter about providing templates so the employees can spend more time doing their jobs and less time trying to figure out color combinations and effective ways to show data. Once a company has such corporate blueprints, it's much easier for presenters to create effective slides.

In Chapter 5, Create High-Impact Slides, we teach you by example how to create interesting, yet effective slides by showing before and after examples. In many companies, everyone who makes presentations is expected to create their own visuals on a computer. Users have access to a wider range of fancy presentation tools than ever before. It is often fun to apply clip art, builds, colors, and other multimedia features. However, a slide can look good but not enable the presenter to deliver its main message effectively. People will walk out saying, "I really liked the graphics and motion—I wonder what software program they used. But what was the point?" Most people in a survey we conducted said something like: "Make the slides simple, easy-to-read without all the noise and fly-in animations."

The title of Chapter 6, Rehearse, Rehearse, Rehearse, gives you a hint of how important we think this stage is. It is very difficult to give an effective laptop presentation using a remote mouse without having rehearsed. It is very difficult to present animated slides with links and hidden slides without having practiced. When you are at ease with the technology, then you can concentrate on interacting with the audience. If you are too concerned about how to work the remote and how to use your hidden slides, then you won't be focusing on your audience and getting them to talk about the information you are presenting. When you actually do what we recommend in this chapter, you will boost the success of your presentation.

Advantages of Electronic Presentations

Sales of electronic presentation equipment are soaring. The reason is clear. Electronic presentations offer a number of advantages:

- The ease of making changes lets a presenter customize a presentation to the audience.

- The ease of using images from the Web makes it relatively simple to add a client's logo, photos, and words onto the slides.

- Visual effects such as builds, video clips, and animations with such programs as Flash maintain audience attention. The results can be a more lasting impression and a greater retention of the message.

- The presenter can actively involve the audience members in the presentation through letting them choose which topic to cover.

- The sophistication of the presentation gives the presenter an image of being technologically advanced.

- The presenter can take the audience on tours of on-line catalogs, Internet sites, or databases.

With these potential advantages also come risks, and we've all seen or been involved in the overuse of technology. The temptation is to use many of these new tools and features simply because they are there. For this reason, a strong suggestion running throughout this book is to *use the new presentation tools only when they genuinely enhance the messages you are conveying.*

Claudyne sent a questionnaire out to her database of 1,380 people. She received over ninety responses, including those below.

Question: What's your advice to someone who presents with a laptop?

- "Too many people try to dazzle their audience with the bells and whistles of PowerPoint (screeching car brakes for slide transitions, etc.), trying to substitute them for quality content."

- "I'd abolish 99 percent of transition and animation effects. There is almost nothing as annoying as sitting through twenty-three text slides with EVERY BULLET flying in one at a time."

- "I sat through a thirty-eight-slide presentation with a white background and many animated images. I was bored after four slides. The whole presentation was about data warehousing and was about as interesting as nasal hair, which I started contemplating after slide 22."

- "The average presenter flashes PowerPoint on the screen and then delivers a message. That's not good enough. The new generation of audiences grew up watching MTV, eating Taco Bell, and using the Playstation as entertainment and a way to sleep. They will be BORED with headers, bullets, text, and corner graphics. Keep them interested with DV clips, gif animations, and interesting sounds. BUT don't put them there just because you can—make them fit with the message."

The task of this book is to provide ideas and checklists for you to effectively use technology in order to convince the audience of your presentation's message. We'll provide the checklists and ideas; you'll need to print them out from the CD or copy them from this book and use them.

This book is printed in black and white. The CD with this book includes:

1. Many of the images, now in color.

2. Four of Jennifer and Claudyne's *Presentations* magazine "Before and After" columns, showing and explaining how we redid three slides.

3. Jennifer's "Creative Technique" articles from *Presentations* magazine.

4. A demo of *Slides That Win: Your Roadmap to Success,* a CD that contains over three hundred before-and-after examples of slides.

5. A demo of CrystalGraphics PowerPlugs. These are excellent add-ons to PowerPoint to create special effects.

Point
Click &
Wow!

Don't act like a machine, even if you use one!

Connect to Your Audience

The title of this book is *Point, Click & Wow!* But the "Wow" is not because your audience is looking at your slides. The "Wow" is because, at the end of your talk, the audience connected with you. They liked you because you spent time listening to them, not just talking to them. Today there needs to be more human connection and fewer technological "let me show you the latest feature" presentations. The technology features should be used to enhance the connection with your audience. If they don't, then don't use them. Presentation slides don't connect, people do.

You or your company may have spent a fortune buying the latest electronic equipment and creating exciting presentations, but it's not the equipment or design that counts as much as your relationship with your audience. We have clients who've been told, "Please don't bring a presentation. We'd like *you* to come and speak." This is due to the fact that people are no longer connecting to their audience. They spend more time looking and talking to the slides than to the audience. Make sure you connect with your audience. Be spontaneous; don't program every moment. Let your audience's reactions determine your presentation's moment-by-moment experience.

You need to be a living and breathing person up there in front of everyone. Show your humanness, and your audience will like you. When you think of your audience first, your preparation and delivery will be authentic. Your audience will react favorably if they sense you have put some thought into caring about their interests. Make this your motto when you present: "First and always I must establish and keep rapport with the audience. It's me they have come to see and hear, not my fancy computer presentation."

In this chapter you will begin to put yourself in your audience's shoes in order to create a presentation for them. You will also consider how to customize the talk.

Focus on Your Audience

Many people are afraid to present. They stand in front of an audience truly believing that the audience dislikes them and wants them to do poorly. They are uncomfortable thinking of themselves as the center of attention. They give the impression of wanting to get the talk done as fast as possible. Such people liked to do 35 mm slide shows because the room was dark and they thought (incorrectly) how they talked and acted didn't really count, since the focus was on the slides. With the advent of overheads, presenters actually had to look at the audience and realize that people were paying attention to them. This was difficult for many people because very few presenters rehearse their talks out loud before the actual presentation. Because they have no idea how they will sound or what specifically they will say about the slides, they may feel nervous.

At first electronic presentations were being given in dark rooms so the unprepared, nervous presenters were happy again. They thought that nothing counted but their creative laptop slide show. They believed that fancy laptop presentations precluded a need to connect personally with the audience. They also thought that the sophisticated graphics, gorgeous colors, and incredible effects would convince the audience that their products or ideas were the best in the business. This is no longer always true.

Nothing takes the place of a sincere, compassionate presenter who really cares about the audience and their response to the presentation. And now, since most presenters have all the fancy effects, the presenter who stands out is one who is enthusiastic, genuinely expresses interest in the audience's reactions, and modifies the presentation content accordingly.

The computer is only a tool to enable communication. You, as the presenter, still have to communicate using your voice, your body, and the positive energy that you send to your audience. Yes, it's great to have a creative laptop presentation. But if you show no true interest in your audience, you won't get far. This interest comes from your heart and your desire to truly meet your audience's needs. Because the slides can sometimes be overpowering, you have to work harder to let your audience members know you care about them and about your subject. In particular, you have to work on your voice. Your voice must sound confident and enthusiastic, and you must pause at the end of your sentences so your audience can digest what you have just said. Also, if you are in a dark room, you need to spend some time with the lights on. Your audience must see you and your gestures, or else all they will remember about you is your voice. But you shouldn't be in a dark room any more. The latest technology lets you have the lights on while talking and showing your slides. But still some rooms have only on and off light switches. Try not to present in those rooms.

Care About Your Audience

No one can make you act gracious and pleasant toward your audience. This is your job and your job alone. Your audience needs to feel that you care about them. When you focus more on the audience than on yourself, you will find that you are also less nervous. You are no longer the focus. When you make your audience center stage and work on keeping them interested and comfortable listening to you, they will respond in kind. Audiences can feel your positive energy.

Here are some behaviors to avoid and preferable ones to use instead.

1. Don't Spend Too Much Time Discussing Yourself and the Agenda. When presenters stand up and go on and on about themselves or their company, audiences lose interest. Usually they speak in acronyms and phrases that few people in the audience can understand. Frequently, at the end, people in the audience still probably couldn't tell you what they just heard. Second, explaining the agenda in great detail is boring, especially when you use phrases such as, "Later, I'm going to show you. . . ." or "You'll hear more about this soon." Those phrases won't engage your audience.

2. Do Start the Talk Right Away. Within thirty seconds of your scheduled start time, you should begin your talk. The audience needs to be engaged right away. Engaging the audience can mean instantly imparting opinions, facts, and feelings about your subject. If it's appropriate, engaging the audience also might mean asking them to comment on and shape the agenda for the three hours. When you start on time, imparting and sharing knowledge you are passionate about, you will feel confident.

3. Don't Read the Information and Be Done with It. When all you do is read your slides word for word, you're not adding anything. Presenters seem to think the most important thing is to spend the whole talk giving every bit of information to the audience. They race through the slides, mumbling and rarely pausing to let the audience digest certain key points. They are disappointed when the audience doesn't look particularly interested.

4. Do More Than Read the Words on the Slide. Display just a few words so you can look at your audience and use your voice and passion to

Position Yourself

Before your listeners hear the value of your message, they want to hear your value. How do you introduce yourself?

The "traditional way" involves facts and fluff. "I'm John Smith. I'm the lead software engineer on the Delta Project. I've been with ABC Software for five years, and I've been in the industry for ten. I'm really pleased to be here with you this morning and to share ideas that my company has put together. This looks like a very exciting project, and we're excited to be here with you."

With this approach, you miss the opportunity to sell the value of your experience and perspective.

Instead, communicate "features and benefits" tailored to your audience. For example, "I've worked on the supply chain software implementation for ten years (feature). As a result, I'm able to shorten implementation time by five to ten weeks (benefit) and reduce internal staff hours dedicated to the project by 10 percent to 20 percent (benefit).

This introduction will clearly position your right to deliver the message you've brought. It defines the value of your experience.

—*Nick Miller, Clarity Advantage*
www.clarityadvantage.com

convey information not listed on the screen. You want people to focus on what you are saying as you add valuable information to what is being shown. You must speak about information that is not shown on the slide. If you don't, then you might just as well give the slides to your audience and save them the pain of sitting through you reading every slide word for word.

5. Don't Stick to Your Standard, Off-the-Shelf Presentation. Frequently, your content will have to be modified. For example, two colleagues went to give a two-day course to a nonprofit agency. On arrival, they were told that the course had only been planned for one day. One colleague suggested they cover the key elements of the course, but the other colleague thought they should just do the material for the first day! Many presenters do this; they never stop to modify the talk based on a changed time frame or their audience's needs. In theory, the whole point of giving a laptop presentation is that it's easy to customize, even at the last moment. Yet many presenters simply don't bother.

6. Do Tailor Your Presentations to Your Audience. The talk you give to the executive committee won't be the same as the one you give to peers in your department. Each audience is looking for different types of information and levels of detail. Ask ahead of time to find out what your audience wants to hear.

Put names and logos from the client's company on the screen. This shows you care enough to include them in your talk. Take time during the talk to find out about your audience's expertise and interests. Put questions for your audience on a screen so you won't forget to ask them. This is especially important if you weren't able to learn much about your audience before the presentation and you really wonder who is sitting out there listening to you.

7. Don't Talk About What Interests You but Rather About What Interests the Audience. One group of technical specialists was asked to make a presentation to top management. They included all the interesting (to them) technical data. They overwhelmed these executives with their world of details. Not only did the executives not have time to listen to all the details, but they were frustrated because they could not fully grasp the details of the projects enough to know whether they should be funded for another year. Frequently, technical people present along with the salespeople. The technical people need to have at least two presentations—a presentation for the executives in the company and a presentation for the technical gurus in the company.

8. Do Consider Your Audience and What They Would Like to Know. In the above example, the executives wanted to know such information as how the proposed project would help reduce costs and how it would keep the manufacturing line running. You can find people who know about your audience's interests. Ask them. Force yourself to leave out the details that are not high priority for that particular audience.

9. Don't Consider Every Question as Being from an Adversary. Suppose that, as you start your presentation, someone asks you a simple question. You realize that you should have included that information in your screens, but didn't. You decide the person is hostile and out to make you look incompetent. Be careful not to go down this path. Your audience will sense your negativity, and the mood and dynamics of the room will become negative. Be positive with your answers. You can be as prepared as possible, but realize that some questions may surprise you.

10. Do Think That People Who Ask Questions Are Genuinely Interested. People who ask questions are usually the most keen and attentive participants. And keep in mind, someone can question your ideas and still think you have given a fine presentation. In some companies, people see it as their jobs to question every detail. For example, as Ph.D.s in a biomedical research company listen to a colleague's research, questions are asked to be sure the researcher followed certain procedures and arrived at the most logical result. The Ph.D. believes it's his or her job to make sure the research met the high standards of the company.

11. Don't Assume You Will Have All the Time You Were Allotted. Suppose your audience has been sitting all day, and now you are the last speaker. You go on too long. You never rehearsed the talk out loud to test how long it would really take. If you keep going, you show a lack of consideration for your audience. Being last in a day's program may mean less time for you to talk. A one-hour speech may have to be cut down to thirty minutes. Be prepared in advance if you know this may be a possibility.

In some companies no one ever gets all the time they are told they will have for a presentation. If this normally happens to you, then only create a talk that you actually believe you will have an opportunity to give. Another factor that affects length is your audience. If they are tired, cut down your talk. If they need a stretch, cut down your talk by five minutes and let them stretch. They will appreciate it.

Customize for Your Audience

Audiences love to feel they are part of the presentation. They become more involved and retain more of what you say. They also realize that you spent some time thinking about them when creating your presentation.

Companies spend hours and lots of money trying to keep up with the latest slide technology. But sophisticated slides will not be enough in the future. An effective presentation will not be judged by comparing its bells and whistles with those of a competitor. The difference will be in how well the presentation was focused on that audience. Greg Rocco, a technical systems engineer of Mercury Computer Systems, has an elaborate, effective way of talking only about his audience's interests. Here's what he says he does: "First, the businessperson from Mercury puts up the agenda. This has been discussed in advance. It may now change due to whomever is in our audience, which may be different than what was planned for. We never just start with the first point on the agenda. The businessperson asks, 'Are these the topics you want to discuss? In what particular order do you want to discuss them?' I start with a PowerPoint slide listing all my favorite customer presentations with hypertext links. But I do have another slide with less frequently used presentations just in case someone mentions something during the opening agenda discussion. Based on what I hear, I make suggestions about what we cover first.

"Now I start with the first presentation. On that opening slide is a detailed outline of the presentation. My outline slide has links to various parts of the presentation so I can quickly get to particular details. Based on what they say at this point, I choose which show version of that topic to present. For every presentation, I create one or more custom shows of those slides. I explain that there are multiple versions of the subject and assess what level of detail they want to know about these subjects. At this point I look for nonverbal cues from the customer as well as from Mercury people from the local office, as they usually know the customer better than I. When talking about Mercury people in this context, I think it is worth pointing out that I am a person from corporate and generally do not have as close a relationship with the customer as the local account manager and application engineer. I also let them know that I can send them a copy of the slides so we don't have to cover every single detail about a product."

On his agenda slide, Figure 1.1, hyperlinks (underlined words) are set up so that Greg can go to any section of the talk. At the bottom he has created three custom show versions of the talk. Depending on the level of interest in the room, he can give an overview with much detail.

Greg states, "For me, I am always assessing how much or how little information my client wants right now. Then I can use my hyperlinks and custom shows to provide that level of information.

"Another technique I use is to have a link at the bottom of some slides, which points to a more detailed slide in case there is interest. I am constantly adjusting my talk based on what the customer is most interested in and where I think we should spend the valuable time we have."

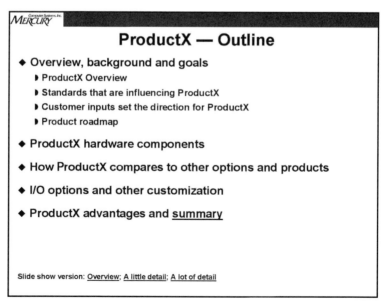

Figure 1.1.   **Sample Mercury Slide**

The above example focuses on giving the customer a unique "sales experience." As much as possible, the customer is directing how much or how little information is presented. This is as it should be.

Many people put the customer's name and logo in the presentation. When you do this, be sure you size the logo appropriately and keep it it's original color. Figure 1.2 and Figure 1.3 are both examples of this idea.

In Figure 1.2, S&K was presenting to Sara Lee. To customize the presentation for Sara Lee, they simply added the Sara Lee logo in the bottom right corner of the slide master. They went to Sara Lee's website and captured their logo. Then they brought it into PowerPoint, enlarged it, and used the Set Transparent Color tool. Because they scaled it too large, the logo is grainy and the Transparent Color tool didn't work very well. It left little red pixels of color all around the logo. Figure 1.3 shows the proper use of a customer logo.

The logo from the website came in a red box, and it looks fine if we leave it. It was also scaled up no more than 5 percent. Look at the different logos on the slides in the CD. You will see the color issues we are discussing here.

Figure 1.2.   **Example of a Too Large Customer's Logo**

Figure 1.3. **Example of a Smaller Customer's Logo**

Some other ways people customize their presentations include (1) using up-to-the-minute data (e.g., top management likes to know the very latest information and trends); (2) speaking only to the needs of the audience (i.e., the focus would change from one presentation to another, even though the basic information stays the same, for example, the management committee wants to hear what is being done to reverse a negative trend, whereas the technical people want to hear the details and process issues surrounding the negative trend); (3) showing photos and giving examples that directly relate to those companies represented in the audience.

Customize Across Cultures

As so many companies are global, many presenters will find themselves presenting in another culture. This is not a time to learn by trial and error. You really do need to prepare or else you and your company's credibility will suffer.

Ask for Advice. Ask for advice from at least two people in that culture. Ask what colors, images, pictures, gestures, acronyms, phrases, words, or competitive references are offensive or not understandable. Find out what type of presenter will be acceptable—man, woman, age, and level in the organization. Ask what the audience is used to seeing in the way of visual content and presentation style. Ask about how people express their agreement or disagreement, both verbally and nonverbally. One survey respondent said, "I present three or four times a year outside North America. I've learned that, in some areas of the world (for example, Dubai, the Middle East), when people shake their heads side to side (what Americans know as 'no'), that means 'yes' to them. And when they nod up and down (what Americans know as 'yes'), that means 'no.' If I didn't know this before going there, I would have been surprised and confused by their head nods."

Acknowledge Them and Their Country. Be sure to open with something that shows you know where you are and your appreciation for the person or audience you are speaking to. Personalize slides to that country in some manner. Put a flag on the slides. Use the country's colors. Find local or regional examples to enliven a concept. Go on-line and look at how that company's presentations "look" and "feel." Downplay the "Americanization" of a presentation. "Slick" may work in New York City, but not in Tokyo or London. Learn to say hello, thanks, and good-bye in their language. Make sure you really know the market dynamics and regulations of your business in that country before you offer advice. Read the local paper. A survey respondent said, "I read three papers *every* day (*The Wall Street Journal, USA Today,* and the local paper) wherever I am. This allows me to reference local events in the presentation and remove things that might be offensive."

Choose Your Slide Language. When deciding which language to make your slides in, consider which language most of the audience can first read and then speak. Another person responded, "I often have to make presentations in Spanish-speaking countries, but I use my English slides, as a small minority in the audience does not speak Spanish. Almost everyone in the audience understands English so they can read my slides. Then only a minority has to listen to interpreters through their earphones." Also, one respondent recommended, "When traveling to Europe, change to some of the British spelling of common words like 'colour' and 'theatre.' This shows you took a little extra time to speak in their words."

Rehearse with a Native. Give the presentation to someone in that country who isn't that familiar with your language. Ask him or her to raise a hand every time you use slang, jargon, offensive words, or colloquialisms. Certain words can have different, very embarrassing meanings in other countries. At the same time, ask to be told if any of your voice tones, gestures, or slides are offensive and whether you are speaking at the right speed and clearly enough. If you used humor, ask whether it is appropriate in that country. Ask whether you spoke about a topic that is taboo in that country. Usually, you will want to speak slower and clearer than you do in your own country. If you can't find a native, try this idea. Run an ad in a local college newspaper and hire a student from the country where your presentation will be given. Have the student sit through your speech and also review your slides.

Ask About an Interpreter. Before you leave, find out the language proficiency of your audience and arrange for an interpreter. Here are some more comments from the survey: "We had a wholesaler fly to Japan to give a presentation to a number of different investment firms. He forgot an interpreter. It didn't take much to summon an interpreter in this case, but imagine the potential chaos attached to such a scenario." "We have had some funny translations occur when the words were translated but not the concept. For example, blended cup yogurt became 'yogurt mashed in a teacup.' Somehow you need to find a way to trust the interpreter and find out whether your humor works, and test it ahead of time. Practice with an interpreter before you give the presentation. Tell the interpreter to please tell you what you should or should not say to the audience in order to establish rapport." "One presenter told a joke that did not translate well into Russian. The interpreter knew this and said something like, 'Okay, he's telling a joke now that isn't very funny in Russian. When I tell you, everybody laugh with me.' On cue, the Russians laughed and the presenter laughed too. The presenter went to a different city with a different interpreter. The new interpreter simply translated the joke as it was told. Nobody laughed. The presenter concluded that the residents in the first city had a better sense of humor."

Remember some of the cultural habits. In the United States, people are used to saying yes or no when you ask them to do something. In Japan, they do not say no; they will usually say "yes" if asked. But this doesn't mean they will do it. Avoid yes-or-no questions. And don't take head nodding as understanding or agreement. You need to know your culture. Ask the interpreter to help you if you are unsure about what type of questions to ask your audience.

Bring Paper Copies. Here are some comments on this topic from our survey: "I have found that international companies are not reliable when they promise you that they will have equipment ready for you. I use 35 mm slides." "I always carry hard copies of my slides and format them for A4 paper." "I carry paper copies as there is frequently a loss of electricity." If the presentation is technical, hand out a definition of terms to the audience before the presentation. This is good advice for any audience.

Use Text to Increase Understanding. Make the text on the slides useful if the audience speaks your language as a second language. This doesn't mean sentences. It means parallel phrases that all start with verbs or nouns. It means organized content. People can frequently read better than they can understand the spoken word. This is not the time to have only two words for each bullet point. But make sure the words are in your basic language without many syllables. Use about eight bullet points with about eight words per point on a slide. Also, audiences usually more easily understand written diagrams and numbers than text.

Check the Translation. Ensure that anything that is translated means what it should. How to do that? Some people who have lots of time have it translated back. If you don't have the time, have a native speaker go through the slides. Explain technical terms to translators ahead of time.

Plan for a Multiple Country Presentation Tour. One respondent advised, "When preparing to give the same presentation in multiple countries, create slides in which you can easily drop in images, illustrations, and photos representative of the country in which you are speaking." In many countries people don't ask questions and interact during the presentation. Plan accordingly. A three-hour presentation could take only one hour if there is no interaction.

Ask Questions

One of the most important characteristics of an effective salesperson, consultant, or technical specialist is the ability to ask questions, then listen for the answer, and change plans based on that answer. You need to ask many questions of your audience unless your presentation is in the category of conference talk, project update talk with pre-formatted outline, or motivational speech to a large number of people. The worst mistake presenters make is to assume they know the needs and interests of their audience and to give a talk based on their perceptions. To succeed in the future, you need to be able to ask questions of your audience—before the talk and during the talk. If you are a "performance presenter" who just likes to give the talk and take questions at the end, your tendency will be to not ask questions. If you are an "interactive presenter," then you'll love the idea of asking questions and building the presentation around the responses. You're more comfortable interacting than giving a formal presentation.

Here are some "before" questions to ask:

1. What do you want to do that you aren't able to do now with the system?

2. What goals do you have that you aren't able to reach due to. . . ?

3. How do you see our product helping you achieve certain goals?

4. What is frustrating you right now in your business?

5. What one "major fix" in your business would make the most difference to you?

6. Tell me about how the system would work in your ideal world.

Now you're in the middle of the presentation and you wonder how to create interaction. No one is talking. Of course, in some cultures no one will talk, but let's assume that, in the culture in which you are presenting, people will interact during a talk. How do you get that going?

Here's what not to do. Don't ask, "Do you understand?" Most people will say yes, even if they do not. What can you ask? You can ask closed questions to find out whether you are on the right track. Closed questions usually require a yes or no answer: "Do you want more details about this now?" "Am I giving you too many details?"

You can also ask more interactive, open questions. They usually leave the answer open and let the responder frame a response. Here are some examples:

1. How do you see this solution fitting into your business?

2. You mentioned a problem with x during our discussion on the phone last week. Here's some information about that problem. How does this information fit with your view of the situation?

3. What additions or changes do you have for this recommendation?

To be an effective presenter in the future, you will need to sharpen your question-asking abilities. If you're stuck about what to ask, sometimes silence and a pause will get people talking.

Make the Graphics Inviting

Why is this information in the chapter on connecting to your audience? Poor graphics aggravate audiences and, more importantly, people stop listening to the talk. They may look attentive, but they are really no longer engaged. Most people have acted this way during a talk. You don't want that to happen to your talks, so be judicious with your graphics. Presenters take pride in the fancy, colored, bells-and-whistles presentations they've put together. This is especially the case if they've spent much time making them. They want to show off their "baby." To some extent this is acceptable, but keep in mind that, whether or not you have a fancy presentation, you still have to back it up with your knowledge about the topic. You have to talk to your audience. Your audience is first. Keep your attention and enthusiasm directed toward them. You will read throughout this book that many audiences do not want sound within a presentation. They don't want bullets and images flying in from all directions of the screens, and you don't want to compete with your presentation for attention.

To keep yourself mindful of the audience's reaction to your talk, here are some do's and don'ts. Know that you will never compete with the real world in terms of glitz and drama. According to *Business Week,* the average American is exposed to about three thousand ads a day. Your job is not to compete with those ads. Your job is to create slides that engage your audience in a conversation about your recommendations.

1. Don't Use the Wildest Template You Can Find. Suppose you are bored with the templates you have been using, so you pick a lavender background with circular shapes on it for your presentation to convince the management committee to give you $50,000 more for your project. The management committee members can't figure out how your subject fits with the bizarre template they see on the screen. There is dissonance among your project, the money you want, and the lavender and circular designs they are seeing. Maybe they can't tie their resistance to the template, but they are becoming concerned about giving you the money.

2. Do Remember That the Best Screen Is Sometimes the Simplest. Use a template that will appeal to your audience and that is appropriate for your subject. Think about what style appeals to them. You may need to change your templates, not the presentation content, depending on the audience.

3. Don't Become so Enthralled with the Beautiful Graphics and Special Effects That You Lose Sight of Your Message. You have made the slickest, most up-to-date presentation. You even paid someone to include video clips, and you've added fancy arrows moving all kinds of ways on the screen. It looks fantastic. You know no one will be bored with your talk. They will really have to keep their eyes open to see everything you have included. There is only one problem. The audience becomes so entranced with the special effects that they don't get the message. They walk away saying to each other, "Wasn't that exciting? I've got to get that graphics package." Not only has the message of your talk been lost, but also the audience never had an opportunity to experience you as a person. You took no time to let the audience get a sense of you as the presenter. The audience will remember the graphics, but you as a sincere presenter, focused on a key objective, never got across.

4. Do Keep Your Message Center Stage, Not the Presentation Slides. Keep reminding yourself to create the slides around your central objective. And, at least at the beginning and end of your talk, you should be center stage, with the lights on high and the screen blank.

5. Don't Organize the Charts, Images, and Pictures in a Haphazard Manner. You may have beautiful slides, but they won't have much meaning without structure. If the material is presented in a stream-of-consciousness style or if you have not organized the data in any logical sequence, your audience will feel frustrated that you did not take the time to present the information in such a way that they could easily follow it. Some audiences just give up. The information comes across so disorganized that they don't waste their energy attempting to figure out how it all fits together.

6. Do Organize the Data! All forms of communication need to have some kind of structure to be effective. Over three-fourths of the presentations that we see are not organized, and even more are not organized to appeal to the audience—they are organized to appeal to the presenter! In the next section you'll learn how to organize your data using the Communication Staircase.

Do More Than Share Data

Presenting information is a challenge. Presenters frequently click through their slides while talking, as if no one were trying to understand or process the information on the slides. They think, "I just have to show them all this information so I'll do it as fast as possible." Here are some ways to stop talking as fast as possible and actually make the information understandable and relevant to the audience.

Provide Analysis, Not Just Raw Data

Imagine that your ten-year-old son comes home from school and tells you he scored 82 percent on his math test. How do you react? Do you congratulate him enthusiastically? Or do you express some other view?

Although your son has shared some raw data, it's not useful information on which to base a decision. If he goes on to tell you that the class average was 89 percent and that only three kids got less than 85 percent, the information starts to become useful. If he adds that he studied extensively for the test but was feeling ill on the day it was given, this information adds a whole new perspective to the situation. You are now emotionally involved and even moved by his story. The additional data provides a perspective that is dimensions above the initial 82 percent data point he provided.

Quite frequently we see presentations with fancy screens used to glorify the communication of raw data, such as the 82 percent math score. After seeing tables filled with numbers, people walk out of such presentations asking, "What did all that mean?"

The Wall Street Journal reported this tendency in an article titled "What's Your Point, Lieutenant? Just Cut to the Pie Charts." The article stated: "Congressional support for new weapons programs isn't as strong as expected. Army Secretary Louis Caldera suggests that PowerPoint presentations are alienating lawmakers. 'People are not listening to us, because they are spending so much time trying to understand these incredibly complex slides.'" One senior official, Mr. Danzig "announced last year that he was no longer willing to soldier through the slide shows. He maintains that PowerPoint briefings are only necessary for two reasons: If the field conditions are changing rapidly or if the audience is 'functionally illiterate.' He now asks to receive all his briefings in written form."

Jim thought he had a winning presentation, but he was in for a surprise. Jim spent days putting together a presentation for a prospective customer. He worked with the multimedia group in his company and added some video clips. He was very proud of his colorful screens and fancy pie charts. As he was giving his talk, he began to notice the prospect's lack of enthusiasm and interest. He wanted them to be impressed by the statistics and the pictures of the product. Plus, one of the audience members began asking aggressive, in-depth questions about his statistics. What was happening?

On first glance the presentation screens looked fine: clear, lots of space on the screens, numbers big enough to read. But the screens mostly conveyed raw data. The people asking questions just wanted to find out more information. They wanted information that would enable them to make decisions.

The Communication Staircase shown in Figure 1.4 can help you to present your raw data in the best way. The staircase depicts three levels of communication, from the most basic form of conveying data to the highest level of suggesting its meaning for the future. This framework highlights your challenge: to use powerful new presentation tools not merely to regurgitate raw data in

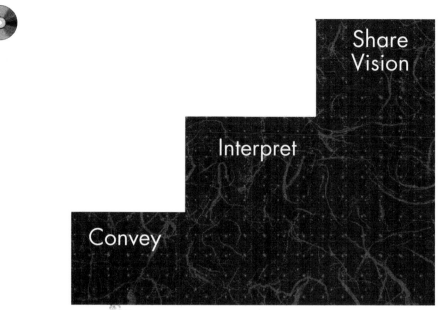

Figure 1.4.   **The Communication Staircase**

fancy slides, but to convert data into higher level communication that will stir your audience and trigger a response.

When you stir viewers' emotions and entertain them in the process, their retention of information will be higher and your presentation's impact much greater. Your audience will be more willing to commit to action and support you and your recommendations.

Here's a sample of how to use the Communication Staircase when creating a slide. Renee Atkinson submitted the slides shown in Figures 1.5 and 1.6 to the Texas Legislature. The slides show what a mental health worker has to make in order to afford a one- or two-bedroom home.

In Figure 1.5, the bundles of dollars wipe up on the screen, conveying to the audience that mental health workers make $7.50 an hour. But that doesn't mean much without an interpretation. The interpretation is next.

First, the one-bedroom home and five homes on the left wipe up with the $10 an hour text at the top. The presenter says that in order to rent a one-bedroom home the worker needs to make $10 an hour. Then the two-bedroom home

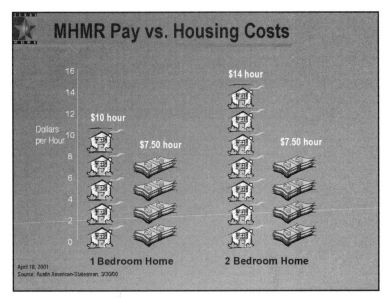

Figure 1.5.   **Slide Showing Pay vs. Housing Costs**

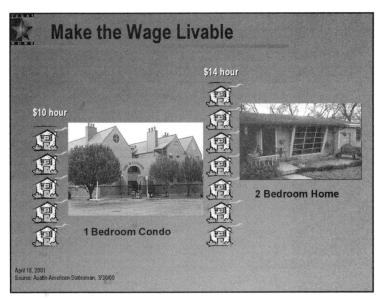

Figure 1.6.   **Slide Showing Different Homes**

along with the seven homes wipe up with the $14 an hour text at the top. This now tells the audience what's the problem with the pay of $7.50 an hour.

This talk is about changing people's views of what is a fair wage. In Figure 1.6, the audience sees pictures of the homes. The presenter now discusses how important it is for people to be able to make enough money to afford to live in a home.

Frequently, a presentation such as this would only show the $7.50 wage, perhaps in a chart. By interpreting the information and sharing a vision, these slides help build a stronger emotional case for a wage increase.

Tell a Story

Look at Figures 1.5 and 1.6 again. The presenter can just read off the statistics on those slides or tell a story about real people who find themselves in the situation the slides are showing. Many people will remember the story more than the statistics. Stories can more emotionally connect to a person and help them to remember your message long after the talk is over. People also appreciate hearing a story when it's relevant to the topic and enables the audience to more easily understand what you are attempting to say. If you can, use a story or a personal experience you or someone you personally know has had. Make it a story the audience can relate to. Use the story to illustrate your message. Don't use a canned story you read or heard from a speaker. Chances are someone in your audience will have heard it. When you tell a story, it takes your audience's eyes off the slide and gets them focused on you, the presenter. Here are several guidelines for telling a story.

First, be sure the story is related to your topic and makes a point. And, just to be sure, start with a transitional sentence that clarifies the connection between your topic and the story you are about to tell. Make it your own story. Chances are, if you steal a story from another speaker, someone in your audience will have heard it. Make sure your story includes these elements: (1) A visual image, either on the screen or a vivid description; (2) feelings, shown through body language and the tone of your voice; and (3) auditory interest, for example, giving both sides of a dialogue can make the story come alive.

Most important of all, practice telling the story to several people before you tell it to a live audience. And finally, keep it short. Make most of your business stories one to three minutes. That's enough to engage the audience and make your point. If needed, use a transition sentence after the story to tie it back to your presentation's message. Here's one example of a story.

> "I was making a software product presentation to an important prospect. 'Familiar and easy to use' was a key bullet point on a slide. I asked the audience's permission to use an example to describe what I meant. Asking the audience's permission is a transition. Audiences also like to be asked about their own experiences. First, I questioned, 'Do any of you ever travel?' Most said, 'Yes.' Then I asked, 'Do you ever rent a car?' 'Of course,' they said. I told them when I rent a car I can always count on knowing exactly how to start the car and drive it. The gas pedal, key ignition, steering wheel, and brake are always in the same place. I am familiar with the user interface. It doesn't matter what kind of car I get, all the user interfaces are basically the same. Our product is designed the same way. Users will not have to learn a new way to surf the Web. The toolbar looks exactly like Windows. Since they will be able to use our product without any training or fear of something new, this is a huge advantage in getting them to start and then continually use it."

Summarize the Major Points

Even when you tell a story, you need to summarize its major point or points. You may say something like, "What this story points out is . . ." or "This story once again reminds us about how important our clients are to us." You could tell a story of how you worked with a client, then summarize the story by using this formula from Nick Miller, president of Clarity Advantage Company. In his sales consulting, Nick reminds salespeople to focus on what's important to the client with this formula: "Nick Miller, president of Clarity Advantage, helps companies generate more sales, faster, more efficiently."

As with any formula, you may choose to say the words a bit differently. Here are some examples of how formulas are used.

Formula 1: Your goal is. . . : "Your goal is to increase your market share." "Your goal is to revitalize your mature business."

Formula 2: We're going to provide you with . . . : "We're going to provide you with an ad in *Woman's Day* magazine." "We'll provide trends analysis of your marketplace."

Formula 3: This will enable you to . . . : "This will enable you to send people to your website." "This analysis will enable you to decide which areas to expand into."

Formula 4: You will gain . . . : "You will gain more sales." "You will be able to gain more customers."

Make It Fun

Finally, you can connect to your audience by having some fun. When that's possible, try it. Some presentations have lots of information, so it is hard to get people to pay attention throughout the whole talk. Heather Stefl with the consulting firm Computer Science Corporation does work for a federal agency in Washington, DC. She helped them create ways to get people to listen. For the last three years she has created games at the end of the agency's presentations that cover information technology and data sharing topics. The example shown in Figure 1.7 is from a game based on the popular ABC game show

Figure 1.7.   **Sample Quiz Game Slide**

"Who Wants to Be a Millionaire?" The game begins with the theme playing in the background and with a click of 50/50 or ask the audience (picture of three people) or phone a friend (picture of a phone). The questions and answers were all in the original presentation's content, so the audience really had to listen. The questions get tricky as the game progresses. When a person selects a wrong answer, the slide gives them a buzzer sound. When someone chooses the right answer, the slide has a crowd clapping with joy. If the person makes it to the "lightning" round, he or she receives a prize that has something to do with the subject matter or something from a local vendor. People now request this agency's talks all around the world. Most people really listen to the presentations, and the subject matter always sticks in their heads.

Connect to the Customer

Let's summarize some of the key points discussed in the chapter here. Say you are going to call on a customer. Here's what you need to do in order to engage that customer throughout the event. Even if you are not in the sales department, you do sell through your presentations. So don't skip this section just because you aren't a "salesperson" by title. Here is what we think creates the type of presentation that customers like.

Call Ahead to Discuss the Agenda. Before you arrive you should have talked to one or two people about their requirements and what the group wants and expects to hear during the presentation.

Do Your Homework and Prepare Before Showing Up. Craft and customize your session based on their answers to your questions about the meeting and your understanding of their problems, projects, and requests. Inform the people who will be going with you about the audience's desires. If it's an important account, which means every account, the account manager will list the meeting objectives, help the team craft the key messages, and select the slides that support them. Create a set of question/objection slides specifically for this customer, with responses. Be prepared to use them during the meeting. Not to do this type of preparation for a sales call is inexcusable. Be sure your slide show will fit with their corporate culture. Keep the graphics in line with their expectations.

In training, surveys are sometimes sent out to gather this information. Figure 1.8 is a slide that is used for the opening of a training class taught by Priscilla Fraser for VESTAR. This is a training slide. The images at the bottom match the seven points to be covered. Surveys were sent out to the learners to ask what they wanted to focus on. The results are reported on the left side under "Your Priorities." The right side, "Topics Covered," lists the topics that trainer will cover. The trainer shows the slide and talks about how the learner's priorities fit into those areas and how more time will be spent on certain points because of the results of the survey. At this point the trainer verifies that these truly are the class's priorities.

At the beginning of your meeting, show the agenda and discuss it. Just because the customer said he or she was interested in "x" a week ago doesn't mean that today the customer is still interested in "x." Don't assume the agenda you created is acceptable. Priorities may have shifted in the last week. Show the agenda and ask what they'd like to know about each item. Ask them what they hope to achieve by attending the meeting.

In a small meeting setting, if you don't know the people well, go around the room asking each person's purpose for being there. Put everyone's name with

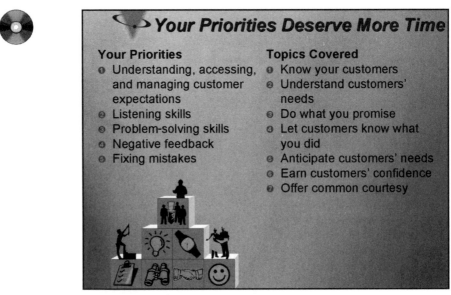

Figure 1.8.   **Sample Opening Slide**
Designed by Melissa Rodgers

their purpose and questions on a flip chart or whiteboard. Refer to the list as you talk and make sure you address all the issues listed.

Once you have agreement on the agenda and objectives, decide as a group where you should start. This is important as someone may have to leave early and you want to be sure you have covered his or her interests.

If you are presenting and your customers want you to start immediately, go along. Stand up in front. But before starting your talk, ask them a few questions to get them talking. Be persistent in getting them to discuss their issues and concerns before you launch into your slides. You may not be able to formally go around the room and ask everyone, but you can ask and you can write down people's responses for all to see. Ask questions and get everyone involved discussing their key concerns first.

Confirm How Much Time You Have. State out loud how long the meeting will last. Ask whether anyone has to leave early. Between the time you set up the meeting and the time you arrive, a company meeting may have been scheduled at the same time as your visit.

Start Talking. If you have more than one or two people, you will be standing in front of them. If you are seated, you have a choice. You can hold the mouse or you can give it to the customer to hold and click when he or she wants. This might be threatening to some presenters, but this is certainly a way to let the customer/prospect/manager/trainee be in charge.

Consistently Confirm Interest and Agreement. As you talk, refer back to their requirements and needs and discuss your ability to fulfill those needs. Before you go on to another product or service description, ask whether they want to hear more about any of the specifics.

Be an Open Speaker. Leave time for silence so that people feel they have time to ask a question. Cultivate a bi-directional exchange of ideas that will address the needs and wants of the client.

Point Out How Your Product or Service Answers Their Needs and Requirements. Be sure you state clearly how your information relates to their situation. Customize your words to their situation.

Briefly Respond to Questions. Sometimes you truly know what the questioner was asking and you just answer it and stop. If you aren't clear about the question, don't ramble on and on. Some of your colleagues in the audience can ask follow-up questions to discover exactly what the person is asking before someone responds. After answering, ask, "Do you want more details now?" Let people know that any and all questions are worth your time.

Ask Questions About the Meeting's Direction. Partway through a day-long or multiple-day meeting, check out what people are thinking or feeling about the meeting so far. Ask questions like, "Based on what we've covered so far and how we've discussed the issues, what shall we continue, start, or stop doing when we resume after lunch?" "What's been effective for you about our session, and what changes do you suggest we make after the break?" Even though everyone seems engaged and interested, it never hurts to check out what they are really thinking. Then you can make modifications right then and there.

Keep a Running List of Action Items. As action items arise, list them on a flip chart. First, this shows that you heard a request and noted it. Second, when someone sees that a request is noted, he or she tends to go on to other items. This keeps the discussion moving.

Summarize with Next Steps and Set Follow-Up Dates. Before concluding the talk, give advice on what you think the client needs to do. Suggest next steps based on all you heard during the meeting. Conclude by going over the listed action items, making sure everyone's issues were discussed, people's phone numbers and email addresses are exchanged, and a date scheduled for the next meeting or conference call.

Some Final to Do's. Add humor that is appropriate. Get to know your clients as people, and establish a friendly atmosphere.

On the next page is an Audience Checklist to use to be sure you are speaking to the audience's interests. Your audience has to feel good about their experience with you. Whatever you are "selling" will not "sell" just because you show slides on a screen.

Audience Checklist

Yes   **No**

____ ____ **1.** Call several audience members and ask them what they wish to learn from the talk.

____ ____ **2.** Ask someone to listen to my talk who will have the same type of interests as my audience.

____ ____ **3.** Speak more about how this information affects my audience's work, decisions, or future plans.

____ ____ **4.** Put several questions on my slides that I can ask my audience.

____ ____ **5.** Create the slides and put them in a file that everyone can access.

____ ____ **6.** Organize my information so it will be easy for the audience to follow.

____ ____ **7.** Have at least three slides and three examples customized for my audience.

Can't we go all these places at once?

Organize
Focused on
One Objective

Because laptop presentations are so easy to create, people frequently forget the step before actually making the slides. They forget to consider their presentation's objective, and thus they create a haphazard, disorganized file of data slides. An effective presentation has a flow to it. Regardless of content, the audience connects to the information at the beginning, processes the content through the middle of the speech, and feels ready to hear the conclusion at the end. To create this flow, a presenter must organize the material around a central objective and story line, use a logical format to make the information understandable, integrate the electronic presentation into the whole speech, and make the presentation lively and vital by changing its pace.

Organize Around an Objective

Although the focus of this book is not on organizing a presentation, we are including a small section here because so few presenters organize their material around one key objective and story line. A logical flow is invaluable for audience comprehension. If you skip from one unrelated point to another, the audience will wonder in frustration, "How does this fit together?" Sophisticated technology loses its value when the presentation slide content is not organized in a logical sequence.

The Presentation Overview Checklist at the end of this chapter will help you to organize your data. Once you fill out this information, then you can create a focused presentation. Exhibit 2.1 is an example of a completed Presentation Overview Checklist that we've worked on with The Nature Conservancy.

You should have only one clear, concise objective for a presentation. You may have other underlying goals you wish to accomplish, but you need to specify one overall objective *before* you start making the presentation. This objective answers these two questions: "What does my audience want from my speech?" and "What do I want from my audience?" By

FOCUS	TASK
Title	Write the title of the presentation. **The Nature Conservancy: Saving the Last Great Places**
Objective	Write a one-sentence objective and have three people agree with it. **Introduce The Nature Conservancy's key attributes to target audiences.**
Theme	Write down the underlying theme or story line that will weave through the presentation. (For example: We add value to the services we provide. With this system, the company's mission will be accomplished quicker and easier.) **Help Save the Last Great Places**
Agenda	List three to four key areas you will cover. **1. The Conservancy's work around the world** **2. Working locally with businesses, communities, and individuals** **3. Protecting the Last Great Places forever**
Format	Choose a format to use. This will structure how you present your information. **Organizational overview**
Plot Points	List how to change the pace of the speech as well as the emotional tone of the speech with examples, photos, and audience interaction. **Show photos, present site conservation planning model, field questions**
Audience Reaction	Write down what you want your audience to tell others as they discuss your presentation with someone. **"This was an eye-opener for me. I'm going to visit The Nature Conservancy's website, www.nature.org, to find out more."**

Exhibit 2.1. **Completed Presentation Overview Checklist**

analyzing the answers to these questions, you can write down your talk's objective.

Here's an example that highlights the need to focus on only one objective. Tan is an expert in water filtration. He has studied it for years. He has been asked by a salesperson to give a technical talk to a customer. Tan starts to prepare his speech. He makes fancy graphs and charts to show the filtration system. He has worked on this system for years and prides himself on being a technical expert. He builds a water filtration system on the screen, and the slides are impressive. He has included all the small technical details he personally considers important.

His objective, one would think from looking at all his slides, *is to share all the nitty-gritty details of the water filtration system.* Unfortunately, that is not the objective the salesperson has in mind. The salesperson's objective for Tan's speech is *to sell the benefits with a little bit of technical information included to support the benefits.* Tan would have made a very different presentation if he had spent some time discussing the objective with the salesperson. This type of situation happens all the time between salespeople and technical experts. It is solvable when they agree on the objective and the presentation is then created around that objective. Much of the drill-down technical information can be placed on a notes page so that the speaker has it to refer to, if necessary, and the attendees can read it in the handouts.

Sharing too much technical information also occurs when salespeople are brought in from the field to learn about new products. They usually hear all the technical information about the product, with very little emphasis on benefits for the customer. The real objective of a product update or release presentation to salespeople should be *to prepare them to sell the product, not to tell them every bit of product knowledge that exists.* Again, some of the details can be put in speaker notes so that if technical questions arise from the audience, the speaker will be able to access the answers. The presentation should be created and built around the true objective, with secondary material included in the handouts.

Figures 2.1 through 2.5 show a sequence of slides for a company sales conference in which new products are introduced. When the product development and technical people fill in these slides, the salespeople will actually

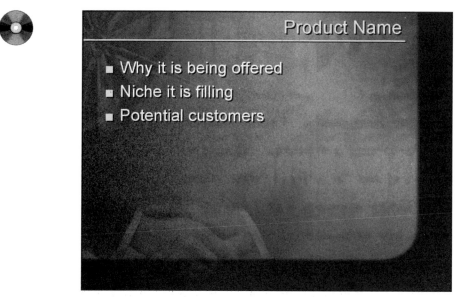

Figure 2.1. **Product Name**

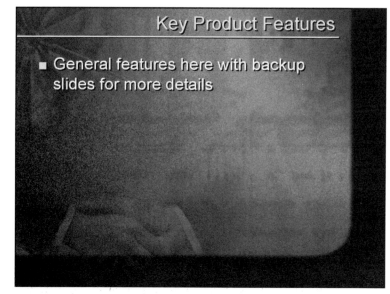

Figure 2.2. **Key Product Features**

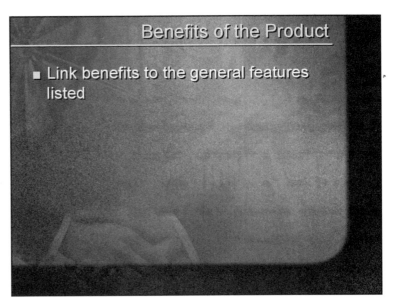

Figure 2.3. **Benefits of the Product**

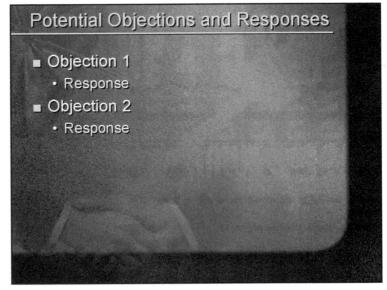

Figure 2.4. **Potential Objections and Responses**

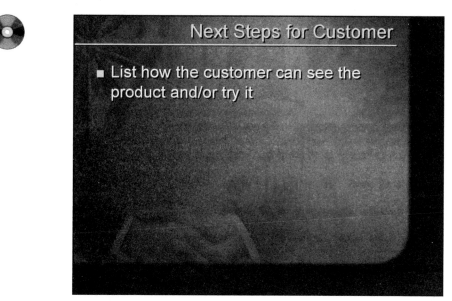

Figure 2.5. **Next Steps for Customer**

be able to use them during customer visits. There is no reason that new product slides for customers should have to be created by the salespeople after the conference. That would be a waste of time.

The presentation objective becomes even more obscure when it is surrounded by incredible and exciting technology. For example, let's say a mutual fund company is asked to give a speech on its funds to employees of a company who are deciding how to invest their 40l(k) money. The presentation is stunning, with lots of colors flowing on the screen. The speech is full of lots of jargon and statistics. But the point of the presentation is lost in an overabundance of details. These are employees who might not be familiar with mutual funds. They might want to invest but wonder whether the process is too complicated. At the end of the talk they are no more clear about what to do than at the beginning. If the objective of the mutual fund company was to get the employees to invest in their mutual funds, it wasn't met.

If the presentation is supposed to motivate people to invest, the objective needs to be *to show how simple it is to invest*. This objective then determines the presentation's content and how it will be designed.

For those of you who have an aversion for filling out charts in preparation for a speech, here's a quick two-sentence objective preparation. Finish these two sentences:

> During my speech I plan to [a verb and noun] so that [a noun and verb].
>
> By the end of my speech, my audience will . . .

Here are two examples:

> *Example 1:* During my speech I plan to present my company's new product so that my audience decides to buy. By the end of my speech, the audience will know logically and feel emotionally three reasons my product will help run their company intranet.
>
> *Example 2:* During my talk I will motivate my manager so that she sees the absolute necessity of hiring three more people. By the end of my speech, my manager will have the information and presentation visuals necessary to convince her boss to let her hire three more people. She will be able to tell her boss how the department can achieve its goals on time with the addition of these three new hires.

Once you have a clear objective, you can structure the content of the presentation to support that objective. Include only the content that supports your clearly stated objective. As you get further along in the process, be sure you title your slides to persuade, not just to inform. Why? You will discover that most of your presentations should be designed to persuade. Say you are showing a chart detailing a machine's high efficiency. Rather than titling the slide "Efficiency," use the title to sell and convince by offering a benefit message, such as "Increase Efficiency by 20%." If you're delivering a training session for managers about doing business overseas, title a slide "Eight Ways to Infiltrate the Global Market," rather than "Global Issues."

Once you have planned your objective and your slides, then consider the type of handouts needed to meet that objective. Nicely formatted handouts can extend the "life" of your presentation. In those handouts you can add details for the technical people. Decide what information is to be given out to the audience and prepare those materials. Print six slides per page. You save paper. The only times you will want to have one slide per page is if you have speaker notes with your slides or if you know that people will be taking lots of notes about each slide. For some technical presentations, you may wish to write extra information about certain slides in the notes page. Then you'll need to print that notes page. It is fine to have handouts in which some pages have three slides per page and some pages are printed in the notes page view, with speaker notes. Also, put a table of contents on the first page with titles of each slide so someone can easily find the information. This forces you to put informative titles on every slide. That way, the person will actually go back and look through the material. Before you start to print out every slide, consider that everyone does not need a booklet of all your slides. Only give them the relevant slides, if any.

The Solution Format

In Step 2 in *The Presentations Kit: 10 Steps for Selling Your Ideas* by Claudyne Wilder, there are ten formats for organizing your presentation. We've adapted one of these formats, which we call the "solution format." In the example shown in Figures 2.6 through 2.14, we're selling upper management on the idea of investing in effective presentation equipment.

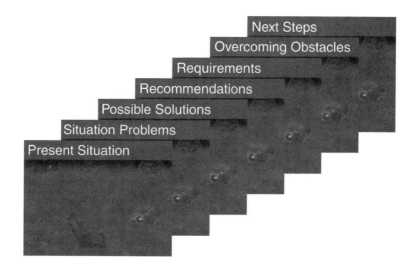

Figure 2.6.   **Solution Format Overview**

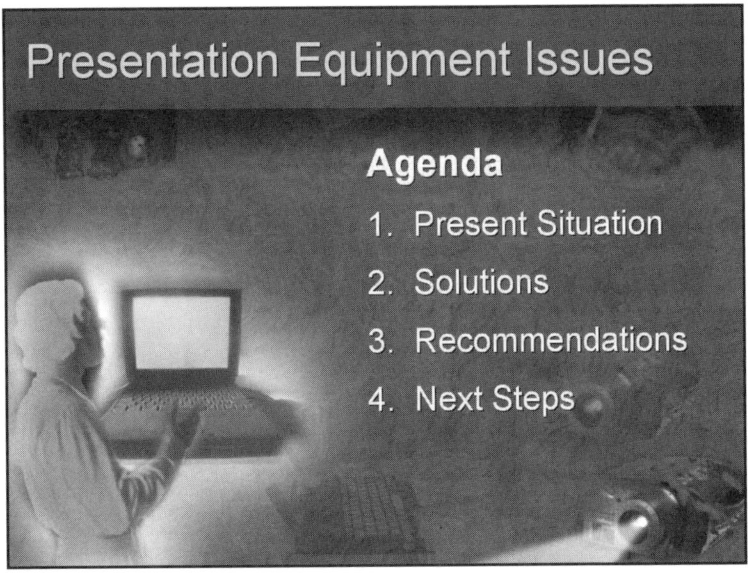

Figure 2.7. **Presentation Equipment Issues**

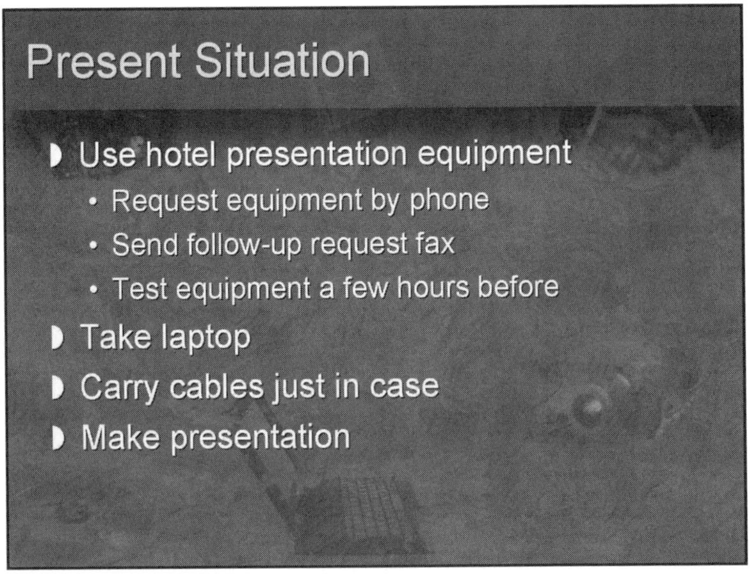

Figure 2.8. **Present Situation**

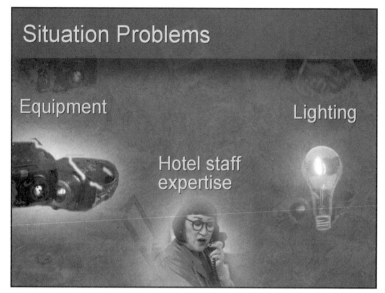

Figure 2.9.   **Situation Problems**

Possible Solutions

Options	Implications
1. Keep doing what doing	• Unreliable equipment
2. Use only key hotels	• Impossible
3. Order equipment from AV company	• Cost, logistics, trust factor
4. Acquire own equipment	• Flexibility & reliability

Figure 2.10.   **Possible Solutions**

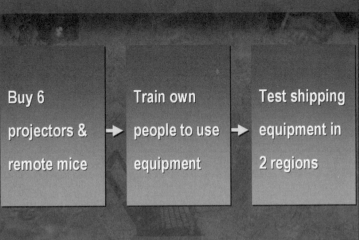

Figure 2.11.   **Recommendations**

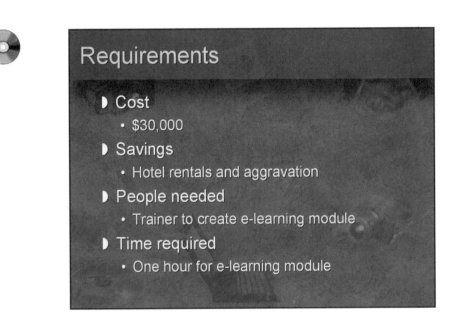

Figure 2.12.   **Requirements**

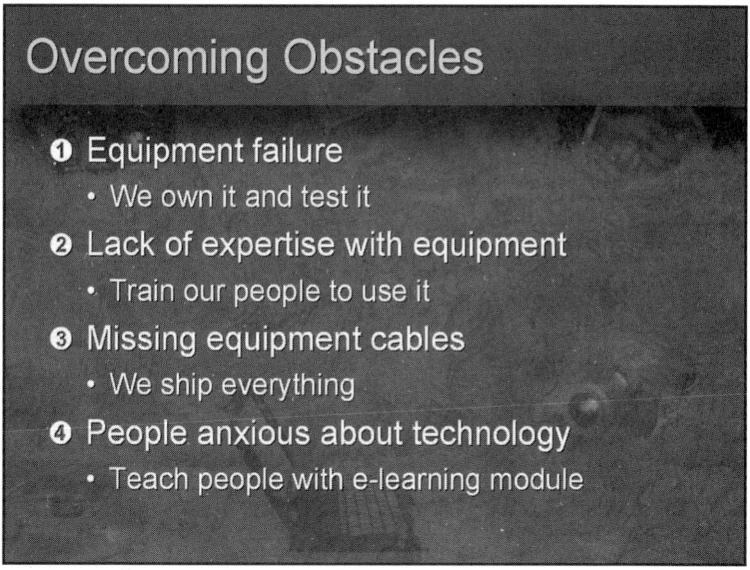

Figure 2.13.   **Overcoming Obstacles**

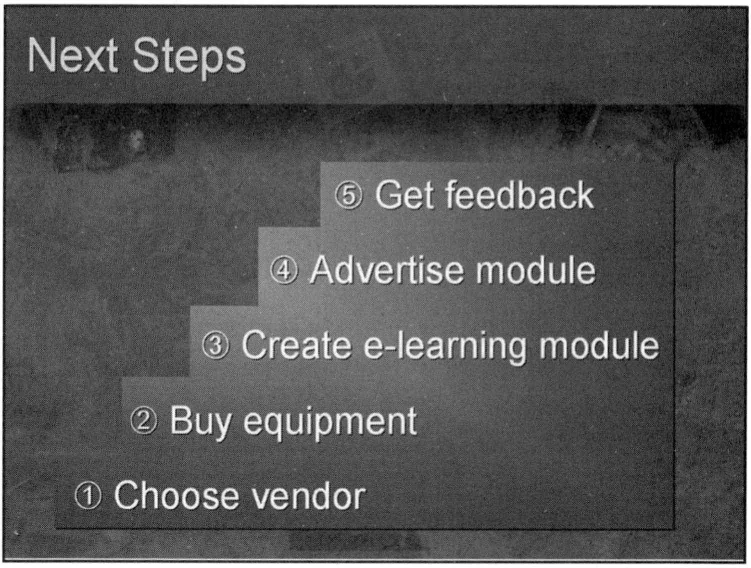

Figure 2.14.   **Next Steps**

First you see the solution format overview (Figure 2.6). Next you see the slides that follow this format (Figures 2.7 through 2.14). Imagine how to use builds to display the information. Don't build every slide. Consider which slides not to build. For example, you could show all the requirements at the same time and this would change the pace of the presentation.

The Presentation Flow

You need to integrate your electronic presentation into the total presentation you are giving. The electronic presentation is *part* of your "presentation," not all of it. You can't just turn on the laptop, give the speech, answer a few questions, thank the audience, and leave. Figure 2.15 shows a sample flow chart for almost any presentation. As you organize the talk, think about what you will do, especially at the opening and closing of your talk. Here's where you can't count on the slides. You will be talking—just you. Also, in the middle of your talk you should stop showing slides and encourage questions and interaction with your audience.

This is how you can use the sample flow chart shown in Figure 2.15 to give a sales presentation to a small group of twenty people.

1. Start without a slide on the screen (a blank screen showing) while asking your audience some questions to hear their concerns and interests. (You might even have some questions on the screen.)

2. Before starting your electronic presentation, let your audience know when they can ask questions. (If it is a ten-minute speech, you would probably go straight through.)

3. If your presentation will last thirty minutes, stop partway through to ask some questions that assess your audience's reaction to the information and whether they understand the information. Also answer questions at this point and stop to answer or ask questions after each major agenda point. If the lights are low, turn them up so people can see you. (The lights also help wake people up if they've become sleepy.)

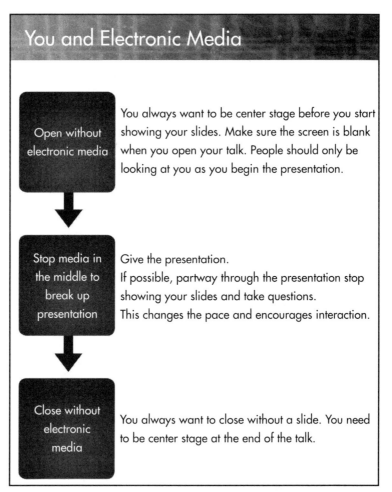

Figure 2.15. **You and Electronic Media**

4. End the electronic presentation with the lights on high, if they were low. End without a visual so you are center stage. Save enough time to encourage your audience to discuss their reactions and to plan the next steps you or they will be taking.

Whatever the presentation, the same dynamics apply. Don't just turn on your media and start. Establish rapport with your audience first. End with enough time left to establish rapport with your audience again. Let them see you, hear you, and feel your energy and sincerity.

Hint: If you are afraid you will forget your opening and closing lines, put them on a sheet of paper in a large font size. The key is to have the points very large so you only have to glance down briefly.

Keep focused on saying what's important for the audience to walk away with. If partway through your speech you realize that the flow you created before your speech is not going to work, change it. Humanness and honesty should prevail over continuing a presentation that is not made for your audience. Be flexible. Change the flow and the order if you sense that would meet your audience's needs better.

The Plot-Point Theory of Organizing

Some presentations just seem to have more impact on the audience and cause them to discuss the content and/or to do the suggested recommendations. Some presentations, even though all the content is there, seem to fall flat. For many of these, it's a matter of reorganizing the content.

For example, Claudyne watched a colleague give a beautiful one-hour presentation that included gorgeous pictures from around the world. After about thirty minutes, She started to get tired. When it was over, she talked about her fatigue to a colleague who writes movies for television. The colleague explained what the plot points are in a movie and suggested that the presenter needed to include some plot points.

What are plot points? They are the two pivotal moments in a television film script. Plot Point One usually occurs twenty to thirty minutes into the film and starts the major action of the movie. Something unexpected occurs to the hero and galvanizes him or her toward a goal. Plot Point Two occurs about seventy minutes into the film when it appears that the hero is beaten. At this point an event occurs that causes everything to change with the hero. The hero's goal becomes reachable. These plot points keep the audience awake with eyes glued to the screen.

How can you apply the idea of plot points to a presentation? Let's start with your graphics. Don't use all your fancy bells and whistles during the first few minutes. You may have the capability to show video clips, but you don't need to hit the audience with everything at the beginning of your speech. You can have a different slide template or background to distinguish between Plot Point One and Plot Point Two. Then add a different slide look for Plot Point One. Or change the way you are presenting the information from builds to showing all the data at once. Use a section slide background to introduce a change in topics or products.

Your speech is unlikely to be as long as a movie. But if it is, you really need to include some changes. You don't need to change every slide, but do consider how to maintain your audience's interest by varying the pace and design of the presentation slides. Take advantage of presentation variety: color, movement, pictures, style, and design. Use sound only when it is appropriate. Most people do not like to hear sound when the bullets wipe right.

What other types of plot points can you create? Even the act of turning up the lights and taking questions during the speech will change the dynamics in the room. You can tell a story that uses the plot-point concept. In the sidebar below, there's a story from the Union of Concerned Scientists. Notice how the tone goes from the problem diseases in the past to the present situation with antibiotics, then to the change (plot point) when the UCS *Hogging It* report was released.

In Chapter 1 we encouraged you to tell a story. That's a good beginning, but you must organize your story for maximum impact. As you tell a story, be sure you discuss all the problems together and then the possible solutions together. For example, The Nature Conservancy tells stories about the need to conserve the lands and waters that plants, animals, and natural communities need to survive. First, The Conservancy tells the negative side, and then it tells how "something happens" to produce a positive outcome.

These need to be two distinct sections of a talk so that the audience can feel upset when, for example, hearing about the threats to the Earth's precious places and then relieved to hear that The Nature Conservancy is preserving such places forever.

Organizations as well as movies have tag lines. Plot points can come from the tag lines of organizations. A single line can be repeated in a variety of ways. If you have some type of theme throughout your speech, at each of your plot-point changes you can do a visual or sound "tag line." Show a slightly different visual image each time, or use words in some creative manner. This is a good

Union of Concerned Scientists

Few of us living in the United States today can remember a time when infectious diseases such as typhoid and childhood diseases like whooping cough and scarlet fever swept through populations. In the 1940s antibiotics and other antimicrobials became commercially available. Their ability to banish infectious disease seemed miraculous. However, the miracle is under threat as bacteria increasingly develop resistance to those drugs. For more than two decades, the U.S. Food and Drug Administration (FDA) has ignored outcries from the public health community to curb the use of antibiotics in food animals. Now the Union of Concerned Scientists (UCS) has become involved. The 2001 UCS report, *Hogging It: Estimates of Antimicrobial Abuse in Livestock,* estimates that an extraordinary 70 percent of the total U.S. antibiotics produced is fed to chickens, pigs, and cows each year for nontherapeutic purposes such as promotion of growth. Already, *Hogging It* has sparked controversy—forcing the government to take steps toward collecting the solid data decision makers need. The FDA has responded to the pressure and antibiotic use in animals is now, thanks in part to UCS, their top priority.

The Union of Concerned Scientists is a nonprofit partnership of scientists and citizens combining rigorous scientific analysis, innovative policy development, and effective citizen advocacy to achieve practical environmental solutions. More information is available at www.ucsusa.org.

time to use a slide that has a different background. The tag line may be the theme that you write in the Presentation Overview Checklist (p. 35).

For example, the tag line for the Union of Concerned Scientists is "Citizens and Scientists for Environmental Solutions." All their plot points in a presentation should focus on this theme, and this tag line should be considered in the stories told and slides shown. When this type of consistency is used, then the presentation gives a consistent underlying message to every audience.

Consider these five points as you design your presentation's flow.

1. Establish rapport with your audience. Motivate your audience to take action at the end.

2. Set one objective and one story line.

3. Use a format to organize the speech. This saves you time and makes it easier for your audience to follow your speech.

4. Apply the plot point theory from the movies. Create the presentation in such a way that after a certain amount of time it varies and changes by look, shape, sound, feel, etc. This keeps the audience engaged.

5. Design your speech as a dialogue learning event, rather than a monologue.

As you consider the plot points you will include in your talk as well as the interaction you want to occur during your talk, find ways to enable your listeners to learn as they go. Create a learning environment during your talk. Use your laptop not just to show slides. Take notes on it. Blank out the screen and let your audience talk.

The Customer Conference

Thus far, we've talked about designing the flow of one speech. Many companies have to design the flow of an entire customer conference to display and tell about their products, services, and unique capabilities. The key to a successful conference is a well-developed process for creating, producing, and

Create a Learning Event

Most presentations are designed as "information broadcasts with time for questions." The result: Our listeners need time after presentations to convert information into useful knowledge. If we design presentations as learning events, our clients or listeners will "learn as they go" and make better decisions faster.

Learning occurs in five steps. These are

1. We awaken the listener's interest.
2. Listeners seek relevant new information.
3. Listeners compare new and old information, comparing alternatives and relationships.
4. Listeners create new understanding.
5. Listeners apply the new understanding in actions or in making decisions.

Use these learning steps when you design your next presentation. For example, begin with a question to frame discussion and awaken the audience's brains. Find a way for the listeners to choose the information they want. Engage listeners in looking for patterns in the information you present. Allow your listeners to actively compare alternatives and talk about them while you are there. (They are going to do that anyway, whether you like it or not.) If your listeners are learning as they go, they will ask you better questions and they will need less time afterward to make decisions and move into action. Most importantly, you can add relevant information that may move them to choose your recommendations.

—Nick Miller, Clarity Advantage
www.clarityadvantage.com

rehearsing the presentations. This approach avoids surprises and leaves the customers with a positive impression.

Here is a basic overview of the steps for creating the slides for a customer conference.

- *Topic.* Presenters are given a topic for their presentation.

- *Color templates.* The graphic designer creates a special color scheme and several design templates for everyone to use in creating slides. See Chapter Four on corporate blueprinting.

- *Format.* A format for organizing the data for each presentation is created. This includes the flow of all the presentations and forces all the presenters to focus on what the customers want to hear. There may be several formats, depending on each presentation's objective.

- *Training.* A session is held to explain the organizational formats and the design templates as well as to give some hints on presentation skills. A completed format is handed out as an example to follow.

- *Research.* Presenters call three to five customers who have signed up for their session to find out why they signed up and what they want to learn from the meeting.

- *First draft meeting.* A date is set for everyone to go over a hard copy of his or her presentation with a manager and graphic designer for review. The purpose of the draft meeting is to ensure accuracy and consistency of information. To complete the first draft, the presenters must (a) follow the guidelines listed on the Total Visual and Single-Slide Checklists (see pp. 165–167) and (b) practice their presentations out loud so they can verify that the flow and words on the slides make sense. If they wait to rehearse until the handouts are designed, it will be too late to modify the slides.

- *Changes.* The final edits are made.

- *Final presentations.* The presenter sends the final version to the person who is in charge of putting the final presentations into a binder or on a CD.

- *Rehearsal.* Presenters meet in small groups of three or four to rehearse the entire presentation. The groups have critique forms. People practice with the equipment using a remote mouse.

- *Extra disk.* When leaving for the conference, presenters are to take a disk or CD of their presentation.

- *Clothes to wear.* Everyone is reminded to wear something that the microphone can be clipped to and a place to clip the transmitter for the microphone. One-piece dresses are not recommended.

- *Partner system.* Presenters designate a partner who will be with them from fifteen minutes before to ten minutes after the presentation. The partners will be available to go for help in case of technical difficulties and will sit in the audience to help field questions. The partners also deal with people who have questions the presenter does not have time to answer. The partners collect the evaluation forms after the sessions.

- *The presentation itself.* Presenters may stand behind a podium, but should use a lavaliere microphone. Podium microphones restrict a presenter's movement.

You've now read how to create the flow for a single presentation as well as for a customer conference. A Flow Checklist is included for designing a pace that engages your audience. Use the Presentation Overview Checklist to help you focus your content.

Flow Checklist

_____ | _____ **1.** Fill out Presentation Overview before starting to create slides.

_____ | _____ **2.** Be sure you have a format for organizing the content.

_____ | _____ **3.** If your presentation is long, plan breaks in your speech to discuss your message with the audience and to answer their questions.

_____ | _____ **4.** Tell several plot point stories in your speech.

_____ | _____ **5.** Create slides and questions to allow your audience to discuss the alternatives you are suggesting.

Presentation Overview Checklist

Focus	Task
Title	Write the title of the presentation.
Objective	Write a one-sentence objective and have three people agree with it.
Theme	Write down the underlying theme or story line that will weave through the presentation. (For example: We add value to the services we provide. With this system, the company's mission will be accomplished quicker and easier.)
Agenda	List three to four key areas you will cover.
Format	Choose a format to use. This will structure how you present your information.
Plot Points	List how to change the pace of the speech as well as the emotional tone of the speech with examples, photos, and audience interaction.
Audience Reaction	Write down what you want your audience to tell others as they discuss your presentation with someone.

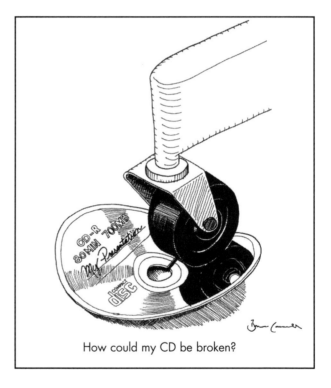

How could my CD be broken?

Prepare for Technology Success

You can have the best intentions, truly know your presentation's objective, and study your audience's needs. But to succeed you must know your technology, at least enough to get by. You want to look and act like you know what you are doing. That can be difficult when you first start to do laptop presentations. This chapter gives you guidelines to use with the technology portion of your presentation. You will also read stories from over one hundred people who shared with us their technology successes and failures.

To begin with, try not to use a software program you are unfamiliar with. You may be in front of your audience and know that the program is not working, but not know what to do to fix the problem. It may be that someone else produced the presentation or that you have minimal experience with this software program. It's hard for people to take you and your topic seriously if you can't even run the software package. Take a class. See a video. Read a book. Practice on your own. If you don't have time to learn it, then have someone with you who does know the program.

The major theme that runs through this chapter is don't use unfamiliar equipment. If you are trying to sell people a product and you have problems operating the equipment, they may ask themselves, "How good can she be? How good can this company's customer service be if they send out people who can't run some simple equipment?" These are some of the thoughts that run through your viewers' minds. That isn't the kind of impression you want to make.

Make someone teach you how to run the equipment. Find out about some of the trouble spots that can occur with the equipment and know what to do. Find someone who has been using the equipment for a while and ask what has gone wrong. You owe it to yourself and to your audience to be able to make it work.

The technological aspects of electronic presentations need not be intimidating. All the do's and don'ts for designing, organizing, and delivering effective overhead or 35 mm slide presentations apply equally to computer slide shows. In this section we will give you guidelines to follow so you can deliver an electronic presentation that people want to sit through.

What's Different About Electronic Presentations

Laptop presentations have many advantages. When the presenter is using a remote mouse, he or she is free to walk around, get closer to the audience, and connect with them. The presentation doesn't have to be static and linear. When links to other presentations are used, the audience's interests and questions can drive the amount and type of information presented. The presenter can access other files with information that someone in the audience may request.

A computer-driven presentation is different from a static overhead or slide presentation in only four ways:

1. *You need a computer.* This is changing though. You are now able to give a presentation with just an LCD projector.

2. *You need to learn how to use the "movement" features appropriately.* Suitably placed transitions between slides, builds, and moving charts can help make your point and enhance your theme. Computer presentations can also include video clips and 3D animations. A dynamic computer presentation can significantly boost the retention level of the audience. *A word of caution:* Many novice computer presenters are tempted to include all types of transitions, builds, and other special effects just as soon as they learn them. The result is predictable. The audience watches a poorly choreographed animated presentation that detracts from its core messages. The audience leaves confused about the objective. Or they may have focused on the new graphic technology but will have missed the messages.

   If you put in animations for text or images, then use them to tell your story. One person told us: "I've seen a lot of presentations where the presenter has bullet points that wipe in one at a time, but they don't effectively use them. At the beginning of the slide they bring in all the bullet points before they start speaking about any of the points. This is very boring to watch when it happens slide after slide."

3. *You need to do more equipment planning.* This is an issue for audiences bigger than about three people. You have to plan for the equipment

you will use. For a three-person audience, use your laptop screen. For larger audiences, the equipment options are greater and depend on the size of the audience, the importance of the presentation, and the budget.

4. *You need to know how to use the equipment.* Slide projectors and overheads are easy to operate. There isn't that much that can go wrong. That's not true with a computer-generated presentation. When problems occur, you need to have some idea of how to troubleshoot them. If you don't, you can end up feeling and looking incompetent and ill-prepared in front of an audience.

Preparing Days Ahead

The key for those who are unstressed about giving a laptop presentation is the motto they live by: "Plan for bad luck!" Here's a list of things to do before your talk.

Buy the Best Laptop You Can Afford. This seems self-evident, but people often discover that their laptop, purchased at a very good price, doesn't show clearly and quickly all the video and graphics they wish to present. Also, bring your own laptop. You may be told that there's a laptop you can use, but it may or may not be adequate for your needs. A presenter shared: "One time I showed up very early to prepare only to wait and wait for someone to find a laptop for me to use. And then it really didn't work that well."

Be Sure You Have a Port to Connect the LCD Projector Cable. Some of the newer laptops don't have built-in ports for the cable connection. Get one for your laptop and put it somewhere so you don't forget it. A visual media department manager said, "Presenters come in with their new slim, trim laptops, but they don't have an adapter they need in order to connect the cable to the laptop. We don't keep those. They are out of luck that day."

Buy a Wireless Microphone. Some people spend their lives presenting in big conference centers and hotels. Since audio is a very large part of a presentation, it may be worth the money and your reputation to carry your own system.

Have Several Backups. First, why do you need backups? Here are some things that could go wrong: You forget the power cord. The electricity goes out. There is no electrical outlet or the outlet is not good. Your computer or the LCD projector breaks. Your hard drive crashes. You corrupt the presentation while trying to "tweak" it on a low battery. You drop your laptop on the way to catching a plane. You spill something on it. Someone steals it.

Practice for the worst scenario. For those crucial presentations do this: In your rehearsal start presenting, then pretend that you can no longer use the laptop. Give the speech using your backup plan. If your backup plan is another set of equipment, that's fine, but practice continuing to speak without the slides while the second system is being set up. Better yet, pretend both systems crashed. Then decide what you will do.

If your job depends on it, you need a reliable, quick backup plan that lets you have no more than a five-minute delay between something not working and your continuing on with the speech. And during that transition someone else should implement your backup plan so you can keep speaking. You'll need a partner who can do that for you. Here are some backup plans. Pick several that will work for you.

- Copy the presentation to a CD, disk, or flash card. Carrying it on a Zip disk may not be the best idea, as many people's laptops cannot use a Zip disk.

  ▲ Make sure the video and other files are saved in your presentation file. For example, if you create your presentation with video then save it to the laptop, you need to have the video files. PowerPoint serves as a stage and just points to the location of the video file. If the file isn't there, no video. If you burn the presentation to a CD, be sure you copy the video file. Check to be sure that you don't have to change the pointer to the file. An easy way to solve this problem is to always put sound and video files in the same folder as your presentation. Then when you move the folder, you move everything at once.

  ▲ Do a rehearsal with the CD backup, just in case you have to use it. Many presenters have opened a backup only to see the dreaded red X's through many of their slides.

  ▲ If you have special fonts, including bullets, put them on your laptop as well—and on the laptops of any of those people who are keeping your file in case you need it. When using special fonts, keep copies of the font files used. You may need to give them to someone else. Also, your links may break when transferred to another machine. You might need to re-establish them.

▲ Check your backup files. Every video driver is a bit different and you may have some unexpected problems, mostly with the transition effects. Check your effects to be sure they look presentable.

- Bring a set of transparencies or set of 35 mm film slides.

- Store the file on a network that you can access. Some people suggest that you have someone back in the office keep a copy of the presentation. The idea is that you can call at a moment's notice and have it sent via email. There are two major problems. No one answers the phone anymore. You can call, but that doesn't mean anyone will be there. Second, the file size may be too big to download through the available network.

- Roger Parker suggests "making an Adobe Acrobat copy of your presentation and FTP'ing it to your website as an unlinked file. Then, if your laptop disappears or breaks, all you have to do is borrow a laptop (most have FTP and Adobe Acrobat Reader) and download the Acrobat file. You're back in business." (To read his article, go to www.newentrepreneur.com/premium/open/open.html. Once there scroll down until you see the article titled "Presenting with Adobe Acrobat 4.0.")

- Always have paper copies of the slides. This is a must! You need to have some notes to speak from if all else fails. We have heard and read about too many people who ended up giving a speech without any notes at all. Don't set yourself up for this kind of experience. A fellow presenter said, "Sometimes I design my handouts so I can do my presentation directly from them if all electronic media options fail."

- Send the presentation to those in your office who are going to present with you. When you are presenting with other colleagues, odds are one of your laptops will work.

- Send the presentation to someone in the audience. That way you can use their system if yours doesn't work.

- Put it on "Flash" cards. They can provide an easy way to move files from one machine to another when on the road. You can use a CompactFlash card, which is like a mini-hard drive for your laptop. It fits into your PCMCIA (PC CARD) modem slot (using an adapter). The cards come in 8Meg, 16Meg, 32Meg, and 64Meg sizes. They are the *same* CompactFlash cards used for digital cameras. As long as your presentation isn't too big for the card (in terms of file size), then it works great. The best news is that it works on almost any laptop.

- Bring two sets of equipment if this is a very important presentation, but also bring some type of non-electric backup. Here are two stories we received about electrical issues: "We brought two of everything—two laptops and two projectors. What we didn't plan on is that the electric sockets in the room would be unusable." "I happened to have the only electrical socket in the whole San Francisco Moscone Conference Center that didn't work."

- Never, never present using the Player. This is the file that you send to someone who doesn't have PowerPoint on their computer. The players are all missing certain features.

- Find the name of the local audiovisual vendor in case you have to buy a cable or connector. (You can see dealer directories on these websites: www.kayye.com under AV Directory and www.avavenue.com.) When you are using the equipment in a hotel, be sure to ask if the AV person will be there to make sure everything is working. Some hotels just have equipment dropped off in the room and it's up to you to put it all together.

Equipment Checks

Here's a list of equipment checks to make.

Check Your Batteries. Use your batteries once in a while, even if you have an AC power cord. Replace your batteries if you notice that one that used to last three hours now lasts only forty minutes. Remember that batteries have a shelf life. They don't work forever. Regularly drain your laptop battery (at least once a month) until it totally runs out and then recharge.

Check the Presentation Links. Rehearse with the laptop and projector you will be using to be sure it can smoothly and quickly handle all the graphics, video, and sound. When you are giving a presentation with hyperlinks someone else put together, it is imperative to practice so you can easily navigate through all the different forms of media. Make sure you have practiced using the links before you attempt to give the presentation in front of a live audience. Also, check your links just before giving the talk. You want to be sure that all the links go to the appropriate slide. If you plan to set up a link to a Website or Intranet and then give the presentation while connected to the Internet, also copy and put the most important Website documents in a file. That way, if the Internet connection does not work, you will still have some documents to show. Here are some hints about making sure your presentation links will work. If you are linking between files, put all those files in one folder. Then all you have to do is copy the folder to your laptop or on a CD and the links will be there.

Check Your Projector and Screen. Try the presentation on the same size screen you will be using. Colors look different on small to large screens. Images look different and can change clarity on different size screens. The most common mistake people make is to believe that what is readable on the laptop computer screen will be readable on a seven-foot screen by an audience member in the last row. Fonts have to be twenty-four points or bigger just to be sure the text will be readable by everyone in the audience.

You may think that your slides will look fine with the LCD projector the hotel has given you. But then you see that your watermarked slides and certain colors look terrible. Be sure to look at those slides with the large screen. You may want to have a test file of all the slides you are concerned about. Then you only have to look at those. You could even send the test file to the person who is in charge of getting you a good LCD projector and have him or her test the file to be sure the slide colors look good.

Video can sometimes be a problem. You must know how to switch CRT/LCD laptop settings so the video will show when running it from PowerPoint. You may see the video on the laptop screen, but not on the big screen. Some laptops work with video better than others do. Said one presenter: "I've used Gateways that run video with no hitch, while the Dell Latitudes that I'm using now, I have to switch the CRT/LCD setting every time I run a slide with a video, which is always a hassle and throws off my momentum when presenting." The only real fail-safe way to ensure that the video always works is to blank out the laptop screen. Use the function keys to do this so the computer is set to connect to the external port only. Then close the laptop screen down onto the laptop. This means you'll need a remote mouse, as you won't be able to press the arrow key on the keyboard. Be sure your power cord is connected.

Always use a projector whose native resolution matches the native resolution of the laptop screen. In other words, if the laptop screen is XGA (or 1024 × 768), then use a projector with a native resolution that is also XGA. If the resolutions are not the same, it will still work, but the audience may see jagged edges around the characters.

Another reason to rehearse with a projector is that many projectors don't support the same number of colors as your laptop. Consequently, water-marked photos and pastel colors tend to disappear. If you have to depend on other projectors, then you may not want to watermark photos.

Question Compatibility Resolution and Software Program. If you are not bringing your own LCD projector, make sure that your laptop resolution will be compatible with the projector. If you are using someone else's equipment, be sure the software is compatible with yours. Ask very specific questions to be sure you can use the other person's equipment. For example, you may bring your presentation on disk only to find that the software program on-site is not a version you can use or that the equipment doesn't have enough memory to run your presentation. You may have to save your presentation in several different software versions. Leave yourself adequate time for rehearsing, to be sure all of the versions and equipment work together. One presenter related this: "After a horrendous experience, I never leave anything AV up to the organizers of any show. I now directly confirm our needs with the technical professionals, regardless of the organizers."

Practice Using a Remote Mouse. This is essential. No one should stand by a laptop and push the page-down keys when presenting. And don't have someone else push the keys for you. You ought to be able to give your presentation by yourself and easily change your slides. Watching a presenter tell someone else when to push the page-down key or, worse yet, hearing the presenter say, "next slide please," is totally unnecessary with the available technology. Buy a remote mouse and practice with it. This way you can seamlessly and unobtrusively advance to the next slide without stopping your presentation, breaking eye contact with the audience, walking up to the computer, and looking for the right button to press.

First, a short overview. Most remotes have two components: the remote itself that you hold in your hand and the receiver that plugs into your computer. Most remotes come with software that lets you apply spotlights and do all sorts of special effects. Other features include a timer in which you can program a break. The screen shows a countdown image so people know when to come back from the break or lunch. Some remotes even have a built-in laser pointer. Be careful how many fancy features you use. In a business presentation, using all these features in front of upper management may make them wonder how you spend your time.

Remotes have two technologies: RF (wireless radio frequency) and IR (infrared). With an RF device you don't have to point it at the receiver that is attached to the laptop. With the infrared device, you have to aim the mouse at the receiver. For this reason, you may not want an infrared device. You have enough to do during a presentation besides being sure to point your remote toward the receiver. Besides, you then stand in front of people aiming the remote and looking at the receiver. This is not a very professional image to portray. Infrared seems to be unreliable in some fluorescent lighting. So that leaves you with choosing a wireless radio frequency remote mouse. But you cannot use an RF mouse in hospital settings. It can interfere with heart monitors.

Tips for Choosing a Remote

Here are some tips when considering what type of remote to buy. When you go shopping, check out these features. Better yet, find someone who has a remote, try it, and if you like it, buy that one.

- *Must fit in your hand.* Some are big and will not easily fit in your hand. This sounds like a small point but it's not when you are holding it for one to six hours at a time. Some people like to put the mouse in a pocket, so if that's true for you, your guideline is that it must fit in your pocket.

- *Must transmit the distance you need.* Some remotes have a range of fifty feet, and some transmit farther.

- *Must serve as a mouse.* Unless you are only doing formal presentations, you will want the ability to use your mouse to navigate through your files and software program. It can be embarrassing for you as you attempt to move the arrow across the screen to open a file. If you will be opening and closing files, make sure the remote is easy to use for that purpose. Some remotes have a track ball and some have a touch pad. So that you don't have to spend time learning, purchase the remote that is most like the system you now use. Try it before you decide what will work for your needs.

- *Must be easy to use.* Some mice are very difficult to use. If you don't do a lot of presentations, then you want a mouse that is easy to use from the first time you use it. You can't afford to stumble and look inept for several presentations until you get used to it.

- *Laser pointer dot must be big enough to see.* Be sure the dot is big enough to see on the screen. Some have such a small red dot that you can't readily find it on the screen. Unless you need to point to specific parts on the screen such as complicated diagrams or charts, you won't need a laser pointer. You can use animations to highlight your key images on your slide. That's one of the advantages of laptop presentations.

Most people use a laser pointer incorrectly. They move the dot much too quickly on the screen. They shine it into the audience. It is an art to use a laser pointer correctly. If you don't need one, don't use it. If you do need one, practice using it. Leave it on one spot on the slide. Move it very slowly to another spot. Turn it off when done. Also, don't get carried away and use it to point to text.

There are many fancy remotes coming out on the market. They have features such as being able to use it in another room one hundred feet away. Again, the key to an effective presentation is connecting to your audience and speaking to them. Be sure that whatever remote you use doesn't distract you from that task.

Tips for Presenting

Use a Blank Slide. Put a blank slide at the end of the presentation so you don't jump out of the PowerPoint slide show view. Better yet, blank out the screen by hitting the "b" key while in slide show view.

Match the Technology to the Message. Don't let the technology overshadow the message. Also, be sure that the presenter's personality can match the slides the audience is seeing. We have seen very high-tech slides matched with a monotone presenter. Consequently, juxtapositioned next to the slides, the presenter looked and sounded worse than usual.

Create a Shortcut Icon. Place a shortcut icon to the presentation on the desktop. This makes it easier and more professional when you start. This is especially important when you are doing one-on-one presentations. You boot up the laptop and then just click the shortcut icon. You appear in charge and ready to go.

Hire the Nitpicker. Find someone to look over your slides for inconsistencies and spelling errors. This is impossible to do when you fix your slides the night before a presentation. You are tired and tend to miss errors. It is embarrassing when audience members pick up errors.

Practice the Shortcuts. Be sure you know how to go back to a slide if you need to when answering a question. Usually you just type in the slide's number and hit enter. This means you need a hard copy so you can see the slide's number.

Use the Custom Show Feature. In PowerPoint go to Slide Show>Custom Shows. You can create a show within a presentation. For example, you can take six slides of a twenty-slide presentation and make a mini-presentation. This can be useful if you don't know how much time you'll get to present. You have your long version and your short version. You can also print a custom show.

When you take time to carry out the suggestions above, you will be prepared for all types of contingencies. You will look more professional and gain credibility with your audience. Now what do you need to do on the day of your presentation?

Just Before Your Talk

Be sure you confirm with your company contact the time you'll meet. Find out what to do should your contact arrive late. There is nothing worse than sitting in a company lobby and having only one contact. Many times the equipment is not there and you will have to find the person who is supposed to bring it to the room. That can take time. Set up equipment. Run through your slides one time to make sure everything is working and the colors on the slides look like the colors they are supposed to be. For example, golds can turn bright yellow and watermarks can disappear.

The Room

Here is some advice specific to the room in which you will present.

Check the Room Layout. Change the room layout if it is not conducive to your presentation style. Move the chairs around. It's your speech. Set up the room so you have the best chance to succeed. Most people set a room in a rectangle, but it should be set in a cone. Here are some room guidelines. Let's say a screen is eight feet wide by six feet tall. The front row needs to be at least twice the screen height away from the screen. Thus, the front row should never be closer than twelve feet from the screen. The back row should never be more than six times the screen height away from the screen. Consequently, the back row shouldn't be more than thirty-six feet back from the screen. There is a rule of thumb for width too. The front row should never be more than four times the screen width, thirty-two feet wide. The back row should never be more than eight times, sixty-four feet wide.

Check Screen View. If the screen is not large enough, put it on a table or chair. That way the people in the back of the room can see the bottom of the screen.

Fix the Lighting, if Possible. Lighting features in some rooms can be fantastic. There are buttons that turn off different portions of the room's lights. Or the lighting can be horrendous, with bulbs that shine on your screen and blur out your messages. Be brave. Ask the hotel to undo the lights that are shining on the screen. In a company conference room, unscrew the bulbs yourself.

The Laptop

Here's some advice specific to the laptop you're using to present.

Plug in the Laptop. Have the battery charged just in case you need it for a little while. But don't wait to go on while running only your battery. Plug it in somewhere to rehearse. And then plug it in again when it's your turn to present. There are too many stories about batteries going dead while someone was waiting to speak. Boot the laptop ahead of time. Here's a story one presenter shared: "I just gave a real-time show. I waited until I got into the room to boot up my machine. Windows NT doesn't boot very fast and I was awkwardly standing there trying to keep my sweat from showing."

Turn Off Certain Functions. Turn off the screen saver function. The easiest way to do this is to right-click (using the right mouse button) on your Desktop, go to Properties, then Screen Saver. Also, turn off little pop-up boxes that say things like, "Your battery is now fully charged." Be sure the projector's screen saver is off as well. Turn off the sound. Most people dislike the sounds of bullets flying in. If that's the only sound you plan to have, then turn it off, unless you are speaking to your neighborhood seven-year-olds.

Position the Laptop and Yourself. Position the laptop screen outside the projector's light path and people's view. Plan two places to stand so you don't block people's view of the screen and the slides.

Move or Tape Down Cords. Position and tape down the cords so that you won't trip over them. After a speech one presenter we heard from had people come up telling her that they were worried she was going to trip over a cord. Tape them down for your audience's peace of mind. As much as possible, hide the wires and cords so the audience doesn't see them before seeing the screen. One person shared this story: "The presenter was not conversant in the medium he chose to present with. He kicked the power cable out of the wall, losing the screen images, then wasted time trying to get the programs back. Worse yet, he showed the first several slides only to himself as if he hadn't yet seen them."

Test Your Power Source. Make sure both ends of the power supply cord are plugged in. Then make sure the power source is really on by seeing if your battery is on. Don't give your presentation off a battery. Always use the power supply. If you plug your cord into a podium, be sure the power is on. We heard about one CEO who was presenting, when midway through the low power battery signal went on with a loud beeping sound. Everyone had thought it was plugged in. So the CEO continued while someone else got down on hands and knees and moved the plug to the wall outlet. Fortunately, there was an outlet nearby.

Don't Undo Once Connected. After you have set up the equipment and tested it, don't disconnect. That can sometimes cause things not to work. Also, if the colors look funny on the screen, one of the cords may not be totally plugged in. This said, some people turn their computers off and on just before doing a presentation to free up the RAM so the presentation runs more smoothly.

Have the Presentation on the Screen. Know what keys to press so the presentation is shown on the screen. This is usually Fn plus the display function key.

The Extras That Make a Difference

Some little things make a big difference.

Find Your File. Frequently within a company the employees present in a conference room using the presentation file on the network drive. This can be embarrassing if you can't find it. Try to go to the conference room early and be sure you can access and open your file.

Have a Backup Plan Ready to Go. If you plan to use another laptop, then have it booted up with the presentation opened. Try your backup laptop with the projector just to be sure it will work.

Keep Liquids Away from Laptop. Keep your coffee or water at a safe distance. Don't let anyone else put a drink by your laptop either.

Don't Share Your Laptop. If you let another presenter use your laptop, there is a possibility that someone may inadvertently delete your presentation files or move them around so that you can't find them. If you must share, you control the keyboard. Don't let anyone else touch it. Also, sometimes the equipment person will change resolution or something else on your laptop so that it works well with the projector. Watch what is done so you can change it back.

Use the Laser Pointer Only if Necessary. Most people do not use laser pointers effectively. With the ability to animate certain diagrams on the slide, you don't need the laser pointer to explain them. If you do use it, hold it still on the slide's images, move it slowly on the screen, then turn it off so you don't shine it in someone's eyes. Also, don't use one for pointing to text. You ought to be able to explain the text without a laser pointer. Only use it to highlight a key number on a chart or a specific box in a flow chart.

This is a fairly comprehensive list. We hope most of you do all these things already. But what happens if things still go wrong? First, don't bad mouth the technology. Just keep going graciously. You picked the technology and if the equipment belongs to the client, do not complain about their system. Tell yourself that in a few weeks your experience will make a funny or instructive story for someone.

Keeping Track of Your Laptop and Its Contents

Safeware is a pioneer in insurance coverage for computers. Here's what they have to say about computers: "An analysis of personal computer damage claims filed in 2000 showed that 56 percent resulted in accidental damage, up from 49 percent in 1999. Thefts—the next largest source of claims—accounted for 27 percent, down from 28 percent in 1999. Approximately 831,000 PCs incurred accidental damage in 2000 that could have resulted in insurance claims. Over 95 percent were notebook PCs. 1.4 million computers were stolen, damaged, or otherwise destroyed during 2000. An estimated $2.1 billion in computer equipment was lost, stolen, or damaged by accidents, power surges, natural disasters, and other mishaps during 2000."

What does this mean for you? It means you need to be careful not to damage your laptop. Also, take precautions so that it is not stolen.

Perhaps you think you are careful. But just one incident and it's gone. A professional trainer and presenter relayed to us that she was tired one morning. She went to a meeting and left her laptop in plain view in her car. When she came out, the laptop was gone. You could be in a hotel and leave your laptop on the table while you go to the bathroom. You come back and it's gone.

There are many precautions to take in order not to have your laptop stolen. Everyone has his or her own system. Some people never carry a laptop in a bag that looks like a laptop carrying case. Once on the plane, put your laptop near you; don't store it in an overhead compartment far from where you are sitting. Some people always carry it into the taxi and don't put it in the trunk. This also protects it from being bounced around. To lock down your laptop, see Kensington's laptop locks.

Do not put your PC on the security conveyor belt at an airport until the person in front of you has cleared through the metal detector. If they don't clear and you have to wait, your PC may not be on the other side when you finally get there.

Almost never put your laptop down in the airport, or anywhere for that matter. A spill on you may not be a mistake. Joe told us that as he was walking to a plane someone bumped into him and spilled mustard all over his suit. He put his case down to clean up. His case was stolen. Some people make it a practice never to put down a briefcase or laptop carrying case except between their legs, with their feet holding the bag in place.

To prepare for the worst, there are all kinds of sophisticated systems coming out on the market every day. For example, there's a new tracking and retrieval laptop system. If your computer is stolen, you contact Compu Trace and their recovery service monitors that computer for its next incoming call. The software agent stealthily calls in with its location as soon as its plugged into a phone line. Go to www.computersecurity.com on the Web. A company called zTrace also tries to improve your chance of getting a computer back. If your computer is stolen, zTrace will monitor your PC through an Internet connection by tracing its unique identification code. If your laptop is stolen and the thief accesses the Internet, an SOS function reports the laptop's location to the zTrace command center. zTrace also has a feature that remotely backs up your files onto an offsite secure server. Then, if it is stolen, you can keep on working with your backup data. See www.ztrace.com.

Plan for a laptop crash. If you work in a company, then there are policies and procedures to follow if your computer crashes. Check out what they are so you know the right numbers to phone. If you work on your own, then you need to know those laptop service numbers to call from wherever you are. Try to call and see whether you can get through. Now! Before it breaks, find out what type of service you have. Can you get the laptop back in twenty-four or thirty-six hours? What will that cost?

This brings up the issue of backing up the laptop. Do you back it up? Imagine now that your laptop is gone forever. How long would it take you to get going again?

Here's one more story about a laptop crash: "I live in Venezuela. I had just arrived in Miami on Friday to teach a seminar on Monday. I was checking my email and my laptop froze and DIDN'T COME BACK TO LIFE. I called the laptop maker's hotline and tried to reboot. The hard drive was fried. I had to run around and buy a new laptop. Luckily and thank God, I had made backup files of everything. BUT, the backup files were in Caracas! I called the Caracas office and had them email me the files and key documents I would need for the Monday seminar—presentation files and some key documents. By 8:30 on Friday night, I had my new laptop up and running. I learned some valuable lessons. First, during an emergency like this I had to relax. My brain was running at a thousand miles per hour and didn't let me find good solutions. Anger would not resolve the situation. Second, I turned the negative into a positive. I went shopping for a brand new machine and I found this excellent deal at a distributor. And third, I continue to back up my files frequently."

Placing Yourself

Stand by the Screen. When you stand by the screen, then you are forced to gesture and speak about the points and images on the screen. The advantage is that everyone's eyes are looking at the same thing. The disadvantage is that you may speak to the screen rather than to the audience. Presenters tend to end their sentences looking at the screen, rather than looking at someone in the audience. This is one behavior that separates an effective presenter from a novice. An effective presenter always ends a sentence looking at someone, never at the screen.

An effective presenter also mentions the points and images on the screen so the audience can easily follow along. Don't pretend the image isn't up on the screen. Actively look at the image with the audience, then discuss what it means. Your audience is looking at the image, so look with them. However, it may be impossible to stand by the screen if you will be too far from the audience. Presenters rarely stand by the screen when presenting to hundreds of people, as their gesturing toward a gigantic screen just doesn't work.

Stand by the Laptop. Some presenters position the laptop in front of them so they can use the screen as a prompt. Then they are able to watch the eyes

Notice the presenter is off to the side holding a remote mouse.

of the audience more easily. It is an advantage to be close to the audience. The disadvantage is that presenters tend to speak to the laptop screen, ending every sentence looking at the screen rather than at someone in the audience. Do not stare at the laptop while speaking.

Many professional presenters have a reference monitor facing them at the back of the room. This monitor has exactly the same image as the projector. This way they never have to turn around or never have to take their eyes away from the audience, as they are looking at the back of the room to see what's on the projector. Usually, a twenty-inch monitor will allow a presenter to see the title and the bullets just fine.

Sit to the Side of the Laptop. Limit the number of viewers to no more than three if they are going to look at your laptop screen. Use a remote so you don't have to be sitting next to the laptop. Don't sit in front of the screen. Put your audience in front of the screen. When you are sitting, you will probably arrive in the office and boot up with the prospect sitting there watching the screen. Make sure you have nothing offensive or proprietary on your desktop.

Notice the remote mouse in the presenter's hand.

Files named, "inside information on Company X" or "inappropriate pictures" aren't the best images for a prospect to see.

Use a Remote Mouse. In our opinion all presenters need a remote mouse. Why? Because (1) you are not confined to the area by your laptop; (2) you are not distracted by having to press the forward key to move to the next slide; (3) you are not distracting others who watch you continually walking back to your computer to forward the next slide manually; (4) you never want to have someone else manage the mouse and you keep saying, "next please," which is totally distracting and breaks the flow of the speech; (5) you can't effectively use certain animations if you have to operate them from your laptop keys; and (6) not using a remote takes away from the impact and professionalism of a presenter.

When you buy a remote, practice with it before you use it. John told us that, when he first used a remote, he practiced by sitting down and forwarding the slides. The day of the speech, he stood up by the screen. Quite often during that speech, he would turn around and notice that his slides had moved forward. He was convinced something was wrong with the computer. But he was just pushing on the mouse forward button without being aware of doing that. If he had done a real rehearsal and stood up, he would have discovered that his finger moves more than he knows and pushes the forward button. Then during the rehearsal he could have practiced keeping his finger off the forward button when he was speaking.

Many remote mice have built-in laser pointers. That can be really convenient, but test it first. Some of the built-in laser pointers have too small a dot and don't really show up well on the screen.

Prepare for a One-on-One Talk. Don't treat a presentation as not important or think that you can be informal and improvise simply because you are presenting to only one person. Follow the same rules as if you had thirty people in the room. Plug in your laptop. Don't use the battery. You can never really plan when your battery might go out. Show the presentation in slide show mode. Minimize the amount of text and maximize the graphics. When you want to blank out the screen, just hit the "b" key while in slide show mode. This tells your audience that you just want to speak to him or her. To see other hints, hit the F1 key while in slide show mode.

Presenting Internationally

You may find yourself travelling around the world with your laptop. Here are a few technology considerations.

Carry Certain Equipment. Bring an international power adapter kit (power conversion plugs) so you can charge your laptop using various types of electrical outlets. Says one presenter: "I always carry a copy of the PowerPoint software on CD, and also on a Flash media card (192 Meg). I also save my PowerPoint file to HTML, just in case I have to borrow a machine that finds my files hard to read. These all fit nicely on the Flash media."

Use Your Own Laptop. One presenter reported: "Some countries have double-byte machines that won't run your single-byte generated presentations. It is essential that you present on your own laptop so you know the presentation will work."

Plan for Problems. Have a nonelectrical backup plan.

Personally Confirm AV Requirements. Call ahead yourself to confirm your AV equipment needs. Discuss compatibility and connectivity issues. Find out whether the images will be projected on a big screen or on small monitors. Once your needs are confirmed, then call ahead to be sure the equipment is reserved. Once there, get help to be sure you are connecting everything correctly. Travel can take its toll on remembering that things are different and you may plug in the wrong connections. One presenter said: "I had a power strip explode in Holland because I forgot the voltage was 220 VAC."

Keep a Native PowerPoint Expert Nearby. Many people have discovered that they need to have a translator available to look at the slides. Some presenters advised: "Make sure that you have somebody familiar with PowerPoint since the menus are in the local language. At an international meeting, I had difficulty with PowerPoint versions that have non-Roman alphabet characters, like Chinese or Arabic. At least with French or German, I can fudge my way around the menus." "In Eastern Europe I had to merge someone else's slides with Russian fonts into my slides. I did not have the correct fonts loaded, and couldn't tell because I couldn't read any of it anyway."

Limit the File Size. In some parts of the world, try not to bring PDF files or presentations so big that you need a Zip. Technology is not up-to-date everywhere, so create something that fits on a 3.5 floppy disk. We were told this story: "A presenter's laptop was not compatible, apparently with the projector. It almost ruined his hard drive. We needed three hours to 'bring it back to life.' His presentation was so big he hadn't saved it on a disk. We had to work from a previous stored version in my computer and translate it from English to Spanish in twenty minutes. It wasn't funny."

Don't Try to Connect to the Internet. This takes very good planning, well ahead of your trip. Don't do it if you don't absolutely have to. At least have some slides with your "cached" Internet pages just in case you can't connect to the Internet.

Learning from Others' Stories

Here are some stories we've gathered to motivate you to take the time to prepare appropriately. Many times taking an added hour would prevent problems or at least enable you to overcome them quickly.

Too Small Type on the Screen. "A woman was giving a pitch to a new client. The gentleman complained that he couldn't read the words on the screen. At the end he said, 'If they couldn't put together an adequate presentation, how will they put together a competitive marketing scheme?' The woman was given the choice to accept an assistant position or find another job."

"In almost every presentation I've seen, there has been one unreadable slide. Some are even so bad that the presenters say, 'Now you won't be able to read this but. . . .' It amazes me that they say this like it isn't a problem."

The Invisible Backup. "I don't have time to make backups. I'm finishing the presentation the night before." Upon arriving to teach a seminar, the presenter stated she didn't have time to prepare overheads. Right after that as she was moving the table around, her laptop fell off the table and crashed to the ground. It never restarted. If the presenter had brought overheads, the seminar would have taken place that day.

If you do make overheads, don't leave them in your office. One presenter left them in his office and had to go get them. In this world, where time is a factor, one has to be ready for all technological failures and be ready to sell whatever is to be sold.

"My laptop died. I had no backup. I ended up drawing on a whiteboard, and the meeting went very well. It pays to know what you are going to present. But now I plan for computer crashes."

Dead Batteries. "I was sure I had just put in new batteries, but thirty minutes into my talk the laptop went off." If the presentation is very important put in new batteries before you start your presentation.

"A presenter's batteries died in his remote. I was sitting by the laptop and I advanced the slides using the space bar while the presenter pointed the remote, as though he was clicking. No one in the audience knew the difference."

The Auto Save Feature. "I just didn't think about what I was doing. I was in a hurry." Sometimes a situation seems to be an emergency. People tend to overreact and not consider the consequences of what they are doing. This can be disastrous on the computer. "Twenty minutes before a speech I was asked to produce a handout. Quickly I deleted all the unwanted slides, making the presentation ten instead of forty slides. The auto save feature was on and had overwritten the file. I did not have a backup file. BUT one of my associates had made a disk of the speech. When asked why he had it, he said, 'I always expect the unexpected.'"

New Projectors. "I bought the latest model. I didn't have time to test it." Just because your computer works with one projector doesn't mean it will work with the latest release of that same brand. "I recently had a color video clip that ran fine on my projector. I then switched projectors, to a newer model with the same manufacturer. I discovered that the video clip would not project at all unless the properties of the video clip were set to black and white. This greatly reduced the impact and effectiveness of the video clip." The moral of this story is to actually try out several presentations on a projector before you buy it.

First in the Morning or Right After Lunch. "I try very hard to be the first presenter on in the morning or the first after lunch so I can run through the presentation at least once before 'show time.' I have uncovered a multitude of errors this way. Sometimes I have to adjust the background of the slide because of the projection equipment. It is easy to do when I can run through it in advance. Sometimes sound is a problem and can be worked out in advance. When I plan to use the Internet, I have my sites 'cached' so there are no snags. If I don't have an opportunity to run through the presentation on-site in advance, I consider refusing the engagement."

Sleeping Laptop. "I didn't even know this problem existed." Most people who start using a laptop learn about the problems as they happen. Speaking to your colleagues and asking their advice and reading a book like this will help you not personally experience as many issues, such as this example.

"I was giving my first laptop presentation, waiting for my turn in class. I got up and my screen was black. In desperation, I hit control-alt-delete at least a dozen times. I plugged it in thinking the battery had run down. Nothing! I gave up and used my overheads. Thank goodness I had them. Later, I discovered that my laptop had gone to sleep."

The Telephone Line Connection. "It works in my office. I'm sure it will work anywhere." "The presenter didn't check the hotel's telephone connection beforehand. He couldn't get it to work so he had to connect to the Internet through his mobile phone. This connection was slow and every slide took MINUTES to appear. It may have cost him his job."

Changes at the Last Minute. "One time with the military, I went there a week before to set everything up and try it all out. The day of the speech, five minutes before start time, I was informed the general wanted the room. We were delegated to a room with only an overhead projector."

"I arrived very early for a training session. I found the room I was told I had. Set it all up. It looked great. I was sitting and speaking to a participant about fifteen minutes before the training was to start. Someone came in and told me I was in the wrong room. The 'right' room according to someone else turned out to be one-third the size of the room I had. Good for five people, not the ten I had. I swallowed hard, smiled, and taught all day. I was later apologized to for the mix-up, but that didn't help the lousy day I had in that small, cramped room. Several months later I saw one of the participants from that day's training and he said, 'I really admired how you kept your spirits up after we ended up in that terrible room.'"

Above All, Do No Harm, Literally. "I was about to present a sixty-slide PR program overseas to a group of sixty-five European product managers. The hotel's technician started messing around with the electrical plugs as I stood over him repeatedly saying, 'PLEASE, SIR, don't touch that one.' He pulled my three-prong American plug out of the adapter I brought, and twisted it into the two-prong Italian socket. My laptop emitted a bright flash and went completely, utterly, and irrevocably dead. All the lights in the room went out as well. After the lights went back on, the technician refused to leave the stage until I accepted his apology. At that point I had already started extemporaneously presenting. My client later said, 'Those who don't know you would never have guessed that anything was wrong. Those of us who do know you were very impressed that you managed not to harm the technician.'"

Turn the Laptop Off. "One time I was using different sounds with my laptop, probably too many. My computer froze up. So I pulled the cord out and it didn't go dead. Someone then reminded me I had to also take out the battery. Well, I hadn't taken out the battery in a while and it was not a seamless, relaxed experience."

The Laptop and Cold Car. "I kept my LCD projector in my car overnight during freezing weather. I plugged it in when it wasn't warmed up and instantly POW the $500 bulb was gone. Not only was it expensive, but I didn't have a spare bulb." Also, remember that very cold cars can deplete the battery charges on laptops.

Shared Projectors. Different people in an office may share the same LCD projector. It is crucial to check whether everything is in there before you set off for your presentation. "I expected to use a remote to advance my slide presentation rather than being tied to arm's reach of the computer key pad. The necessary items were not put back in the box by the last user."

Transferring to Another Computer. Don't make a file that is impossible to copy. "One person had an eighteen-slide presentation with pictures stored at a very high resolution. He couldn't fit it on a floppy disk. In fact I don't think it would have fit on a 100MB Zip disk."

The Fireworks Crash. "I was doing a presentation when the audience, spontaneously, began to mumble elongated ohhhs and ahhhs. I turned around to view the screen, as I knew my presentation was not worthy of the ohhhs and ahhhs one would hear during fireworks. My laptop was in the process of crashing and in a blaze of glory it went out with a dramatic 'light show.'"

The Promised Projector. "We were out of town trying to use someone else's projector. We could not get our laptop to project. After fiddling with it, and people waiting, we briefed with our hard copy. We were a little embarrassed." This is a no-win situation. Even if their projector is old or not working, it is not useful to start a presentation by telling the client that they have lousy or outdated equipment.

Check Where You Are Writing. If you use a screen and whiteboard interchangeably, don't accidentally sketch or write on the screen, especially with a permanent marker. "I couldn't believe I did it. I wrote with my marker on the screen."

Projection Venue. "I practiced my presentation standing by a screen. When I saw the room, everyone had a monitor. I was thrown off. Instead of saying, 'Now look here at how this system fits together,' I needed to say, 'As you see on your monitor, the system fits together. . . .'"

Live Internet. "Once I was using the live Internet connection and the line went down. I didn't have a backup. Never again! I can now give my presentation without a live Internet connection."

Disappearing Slides. "I prepared a presentation on my company's mapped drive. When I got to the client's, the file was not on the drive."

Checked Equipment. If you do have to check the equipment on an airplane, be sure you have the right kind of box for it. And, as soon as you arrive, test it out. "I had to fly on a prop plane and they forced me to check my LCD projector. When I went to set it up, the projector was shot. I didn't have transparencies, but that wouldn't have mattered. The hotel's one and only overhead projector was broken!"

Copying Handouts to Give Out. If you need to use your handouts, don't erase your presentation notes to yourself until you make a copy of them. "We were forced to make overheads in the middle of a meeting. One colleague erased some handwritten notes that were on the hard-copy slides and this threw the other presenter for a loop."

When the Stakes Are High, Pack Your Own Equipment. Don't trust what people say they will have in terms of equipment. If you have to, rent what you need, if you can't, at least find out as soon as you can what equipment is actually available. "The setting was a surgery resident research competition. Each resident had a maximum of ten minutes to present, then with five minutes for questions. Time was tight. One resident brought a CD, but the computer didn't have a CD-ROM. After twenty minutes with no laptop with a CD, the resident was told his time was up. The next day I privately saw his presentation about his research. His research was fantastic. I was one of the judges and would have certainly given the resident first prize; not to mention many chairs of departments would have been interested in recruiting him. This simple mistake may prove to be a career-crippling problem."

Plan for Delayed Flights. "*Problem 1:* We had a wholesaler who flew to his destination only to arrive several hours later than planned. *Problem 2:* He had checked his laptop and discovered at the hotel that he had a huge hole through the screen. *Problem 3:* He had fifteen minutes to get to the meeting and he had no backup, no overheads, no hard copy, nothing. *Problem 4:* He attempted to persuade fifty brokers to sell our products with zero slides, zero handouts, and no map to guide his presentation. *Problem 5:* How to go back and convince the brokers that the products really are excellent."

The 70MB Presentation. "The presenter had a 70MB file. Just when he started, some mini-electrical shortcut made his laptop reboot. The audience had to wait fifteen minutes for the presentation to re-appear."

The Future of Technology

We asked Gary Kayye, CTS, to give us a vision of what's coming for technology. Gary is chief visionary of Kayye Consulting, a firm that specializes in providing marketing consulting and training development to the professional audiovisual (ProAV) industry. He can be reached at www.kayye.com or via email at gkayye@kayye.com. Here's his vision.

What's Next for the Road Warrior

Well, believe it or not, in the not-too-distant future, you'll be carrying around a projector that weighs less than your laptop—a lot less. Yes, even one of those skinny, slim-top computers.

Projector manufacturers are readying new silicon technology that will dramatically shrink the size of the portable projector. Currently the micro-portables weigh in at just under three pounds. The projectors will use an internal imager called a DMD (digital micro-mirror device) that is housed on silicon and contains hundreds of thousands of tiny mirrors rocking back and forth to reflect colored light through the projector's lens and onto the screen. Texas Instruments is working toward introducing a 1.5-pound projector (yes, 1.5 pounds) at the end of 2001. That's small! You'll find it easier to carry the projector and your laptop anywhere you go. You won't have to worry about checking it. Everything will be so small.

But, there's more. A host of projector manufacturers are now rolling out projectors with network integration. But that's not the real news. The real news is that to make the networkable (capable of connecting to a corporate LAN or WAN) projector, the manufacturers are adding in little-bitty computers (pocket PCs) to process files, play files, save files, etc. You are now actually able to project a presentation *without* a laptop attached. How? You send the PowerPoint file to the projector (like you do to print a presentation on a printer) and then play it from the projector itself. The projectors have either memory cards or a small hard drive for memory. Some even hold up to 128Meg memory cards. This will be useful for those of you who don't need to customize, add to, or change your speech just before or during a presentation.

Finally, along with the rest of the world, they're going digital. Today, presentations are projected via analog cables connected from a laptop to a projector. Since it's analog, there are a lot of little, annoying adjustments that you have to make on a projector to get the image to "lock up" seamlessly (that is, phase, clock, timing, shift, etc.). Well, with the advent and adoption of the digital video standard DVI (digital visual interface), all the computer manufacturers have standardized on a single transmission protocol for sending video signals to monitors and projectors. A computer with DVI connected to a projector with DVI means that by merely connecting the cable to the projector, all the projector's controls are automatically configured through the DVI timing connector pin. Thus, setup time is virtually eliminated, as all you'll have to do is simply connect the computer to the projector, and the projector will recognize the computer and match the laptop resolution and color-bit depth. One other advantage is that you will no longer have to push certain keys to get the computer to show your slides on the screen.

—Gary Kayye, Kayye Consulting
www.kayye.com

The Ideal World

In our ideal technology world, the presenter would carry everything. If it were really ideal, someone else would carry it and the presenter would tag along! But as that's impossible, we suggest you go for the lighter equipment. The presenter would have a laptop, a remote mouse, and an LCD projector. That way the presenter is used to the equipment, knows it works, and, over time, will have experience with how to use it. And the novice presenter would have two hot-line numbers to call for the just-in-case situations.

Use the following Technology Checklist and Equipment Checklist to prepare ahead of time and on-site. Also, for your next trip decide which equipment you need to carry. Make your own list to use for every trip. Never depend on your memory when packing equipment.

Technology Checklist

Preparation Ahead of Time

Yes | **No**

_____ | _____ *Make air travel bearable.* Get pre-assigned seats. It's hard to work on your laptop when sitting in a middle seat. Some people like the aisle on day flights as there is more leg room. They like the window on night flights so that people aren't stepping over them as they try to sleep. Stay away from the seats by the lavatory.

_____ | _____ *Get in right hotel.* Ask for local advice on where to stay. Some hotels have the same name. Be sure you were booked in the right one. Have a room on the top floor so you won't be disturbed by traffic noise.

_____ | _____ *Back up laptop's hard drive.* Imagine the worst. Your laptop is stolen. Then back it up before you leave.

_____ | _____ *Back up the presentation.* Plan for the worst and have several back-up plans ready. Be sure you copy all the related or linked files (video clips, flash animations).

_____ | _____ *Load other materials.* If you're selling you may need product spec sheets, price lists, product photos, etc.

_____ | _____ *Store key information.* Put all key information in one place: access numbers, credit card numbers, other remote-access information, laptop emergency help number. Some people pre-program it on their laptops.

_____ | _____ *Carry key items.* Have a list of items you must carry. Be sure you have all of them.

_____ | _____ *Confirm the room layout.* Speak to the person who will help you with the room layout when you arrive. Be sure there are enough chairs. Ask how the lighting is set up.

(Continued)

Preparation Ahead of Time (*Continued*)

Yes **No**

_____ _____ *Confirm you'll have time to rehearse in the room.* Request that you be given time to set up and rehearse your speech. Your goal is to have room access before your audience arrives.

_____ _____ *Confirm your technology needs.* Find out where the screen is placed and where you will need to stand.

_____ _____ *Know the local AV vendor.* If you are on your own, be sure you have a number to call in case you are desperate.

_____ _____ *Set up shortcuts on desktop.* Some people like to create shortcut folders on the desktop so it's easy to access their presentation.

Preparation on Arrival

Yes **No**

_____ _____ *Test equipment.* Be sure power cords are working. Don't use battery. Make sure lights don't shine directly on the screen. Make sure everyone will be able to see the screen. Test your sound, if using. Hide and/or tape all the technology cords.

_____ _____ *Rehearse with the projector.* Rehearse with the projector and the screen size you will use so you can view the color combinations and video clips on the projector.

_____ _____ *Turn off screen saver.* Check to be sure the screen saver is also turned off on the projector.

_____ _____ *Redo the room layout.* No matter what you send people, it seems you have to rearrange the room. Allow time for that.

_____ _____ *Check microphones.* Be sure the sound works well.

_____ _____ *Check the lighting.* Make sure you know how to make the lighting work the best for the room.

(Continued)

Preparation on Arrival (*Continued*)

Yes No

____ ____ *Find the restrooms.* This is important for you, but also in case someone in your audience asks for directions.

____ ____ *Have water handy.* Put a glass of water where you will be speaking, just not too close to the laptop.

____ ____ *Check clothing.* Be sure everything is buttoned, zipped, etc. Who knows what may have occurred as you set up the equipment.

____ ____ *Assign people.* Ask people to be in charge of the room temperature, the lighting, and the back-up plan implementation.

During the Speech

Yes No

____ ____ *Reboot.* When you are presenting all day, reboot during breaks or as often as possible to clear memory.

____ ____ *Use remote mouse.* Keep the mouse in your hand by your side and gesture with the other hand.

____ ____ *Drink water.* Keep yourself hydrated and energized by drinking water.

After the Speech

Yes No

____ ____ *Take out everything you brought in.* You may be tired. Double check to be sure you have collected everything. There is nothing worse than leaving your power cord in some company's conference room and having to go back hours later trying to convince the cleaning people to let you in.

Equipment Checklist

Need **Don't Need**

1. Laptop with power cord and user's book—at least the pages you might need

2. Extra battery for laptop

3. Remote mouse with remote control cable and extra batteries

4. LCD projector with power cord, lens cap, and cable for connecting to the laptop and direction booklet

5. Extra bulb for LCD projector

6. Pointer with extra batteries

7. Power strip with long extension cord

8. Duct or electrical tape to tape down cords

9. Screen

10. Phone and phone cord, palm pilot, printer

11. CD-ROM and floppy drives

12. Adapters, surge protector, etc., for international travel

This slide is really going to explain
our company.

Design
Corporate
Blueprints

Many presentations today don't look professional, nor do they always convey the appropriate messages. Yet people have spent hours, even days, creating them. For the amount of time spent, the return is just not there. Unfortunately, people do not receive the tools or appropriate training in order to create professional, audience-centered slides. Someone may say, "We send our employees to PowerPoint training." That is only training in the features of the software. Most software courses do not teach how to *use* the features to create effective slides. Although most people realize the need for improvement, they aren't sure what to do.

The underlying problem is that companies don't give their employees the files, that is, PowerPoint or other software program files, that they need in order to create effective presentation slides. Typically, a company will create one slide background look and send it out, telling employees that this is the background they all have to use. The company typically believes that this one background is enough for all the presentations the company delivers. Unfortunately, that's not true. First, it's boring for an audience to see just one slide look. Usually that slide look consists of bulleted phrases. Customer and vendor conferences can be one or two days in length. No one wants to sit looking at the same blue background with the seven bulleted phrases on each slide for twelve hours. Frequently, the background doesn't really work for every slide. For example, a dark blue patterned background isn't the best to use when showing many charts and intricate diagrams.

Why do companies operate in this manner? Companies do this because they are functionally organized. Here's one scenario that occurs in many companies: One person in a designated graphics department creates the background look. This look may or may not work for the type of information that has to be put on the slides. Someone else in the marketing department creates the slides for the new product launch. And then a salesperson actually gives the presentation to the customer. These people don't work together. They operate in a vacuum. They are not concerned about the customer's reaction to the presentation's length, design, or information. Their performance ratings have nothing to do with the customer's reaction. Even more upsetting, they think they know better than the salesperson and try to demand that the salesperson give the presentation exactly as it was created. Since presentation slides are able to be redone, this is good news for most salespeople, as they frequently have to redo the slides sent to them.

We have one simple solution. Companies need corporate blueprints. What is a corporate blueprint? A corporate blueprint includes presentation formats (see the sales format, pp. 37–39) and ten to twenty different slide designs companies need in order to present a unique, branded image externally to their customers and internally to their employees. In this chapter you will see some design slides.

Every company needs to design a special look and feel that gives the world an impression of its strength, talents, and focus. Many companies do that very well with printed materials, such as their annual report or brochures. Most do not do it well with presentations delivered electronically.

What are the steps in creating a corporate blueprint?

Step 1: Create Company Formats. Formats, or outlines, need to be created for the specific type of presentations given most frequently. First, the presenter decides on the presentation's objective and key message or story line. Then a format is chosen to help organize and craft the content for the message. Here are several formats many companies could use: (a) product launch format; (b) company overview format; (c) product sales format; (d) strategy recommendation format; (e) project update format; and (f) technical update format. These formats need to be created and tested by the people who will be using them. Many presentation software packages include formats in the software, but in all likelihood companies will want to customize them.

Step 2: Design Slides with a Background Look. First, a background look will be designed, then slides will be designed to go with that background. To decide what different design looks are needed, first, watch how the information is presented now. Then create slide looks to make the information more "digestible" to the audience. For example, when a new product is introduced, a slide comparing some other product in the market to this new product can be created. This comparison slide design can be one of the slides for that new product's format.

Also, slide designs should enable the presenter to interact with the audience, unless the speech is to a very large audience. Presentations need to be created in such a way that audience involvement occurs. The easier it is for a presenter to discuss the slide, the more likely the presenter will look at the audience and engage in a dialogue, versus a monologue. Tables that compare products or project phases, before-and-after photos, questions on slides, and fill-in-the-information slides all help the presenter engage with the audience. You'll see some of these examples and more later in this chapter.

Benefits of Corporate Blueprinting

Many benefits accrue from corporate blueprinting. They are described below.

Time Savings. When people don't have to start from scratch, they will save hours. For example, in many companies, if a technical person needs a comparison slide without a blue background, he has to create such a slide. He will save time if that type of slide is already in existence.

Consistent Corporate Image and Message. The second benefit is that the company will have one corporate image in the marketplace. With a pre-defined color scheme and many different slide designs, the slides will be easy to mix and match between presentations. People will look forward to using all the different designs and not go off on their own, either creating horrid color combinations or just giving up and creating text slide after text slide. With a consistent corporate image, the presentations will—just by their structure and design—subtly tell audiences about the mission and goals of the company.

Higher Standards of Professionalism. Companies will have professional looking slides for their presentations, showing their audiences that they took the time and energy to create well-conceived slide designs.

Ability to Focus on Other Business Concerns. The fourth benefit is that people will be able to spend more time on the real work of creating the company's future. The businessperson can think about larger issues of business expansion and customer satisfaction.

Ease of Delivery. Presenters will be more interested in speaking if they don't have to look at the same slide design hour after hour. Variety in the slides enables the presenter to have more variety in voice tone, gestures, and audience interaction.

If you want your company presenters to be smarter about creating and delivering presentations, then provide a library of formats and slide designs that employees can use to create professional and consistent slides for their presentations. Figure 4.1 is a flow chart of how the blueprint process fits into the whole scheme of a presentation. Next are some examples of actual company

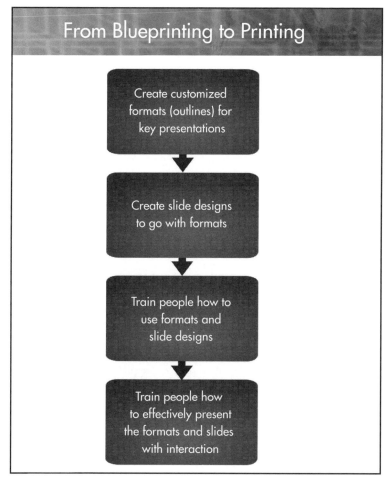

Figure 4.1.   **Flow Chart of Blueprinting Process**

blueprints from Summit Business Consulting, The Nature Conservancy, and Harmon, Inc. To see these designs in color, open the CD and look at them.

Training Example: Summit Business Consulting Inc.

Summit Business Consulting Inc. has an unusually high need for presentation graphics. Summit develops custom education and training materials as well as facilitates strategic planning, team building, and BEST manufacturing practices. Fletcher Birmingham, the president, told us that they give their own presentations to clients, but they also create training slide shows for clients who then use them in their companies. Consequently, their slide designs had to be effective, but simple enough so that most of their clients could use them in their own companies. Fletcher didn't want to be designing new templates for every new training package for a client. He also wanted some ideas to use over and over again with different training subjects. To address Summit's needs, we created one master background template with varied slide designs throughout. The master background carries the same design theme throughout the presentation.

Because Fletcher was creating presentations that his different clients would present, we created a space for his clients' logos. He needed a space dedicated to training images and a space for the client's logo. He said he would probably download his clients' logos from the Internet, where most of these logos have a white box around them. To make it easy for him, we created "white logo" space on the right of the slide.

The training sessions are divided into three to four concepts. The seminars are created so the client can teach it in the client's company. To make it easier for the trainer to not have to memorize the information, the key concepts are all discussed and shown at the beginning of the class. Then each concept is explained in detail with exercises and discussion questions. Notice the concept icons on the bottom left of several slides. Each icon tells the audience and reminds the presenter which concept is being discussed. Many different icons, images, or photos could be put in this corner to keep reminding the audience which topic is being discussed.

The sample slides from Summit are shown in Figures 4.2 through 4.13 with actual content plugged in. The Nature Conservancy and Harmon slides shown later are simply blueprints, without actual content.

Figure 4.2. **Opening Slide for Summit Consulting**

Figure 4.2 shows the slide to be used when Summit presents. For the presentations that are given to clients, the first slide will be the client's business images.

Figure 4.3. **Summit Text Slide**

Figure 4.3 is a text slide with bullets and fonts set up to be a certain size and look. Use Arial Narrow font to have space for longer titles.

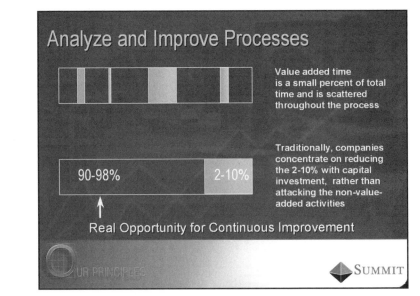

Figure 4.4. **Summit First Agenda Item**

Figure 4.4 is the first agenda image. The training program is organized around three agenda points with images. The big image on this slide is reduced and put in the lower left-hand corner whenever that section of the agenda is discussed.

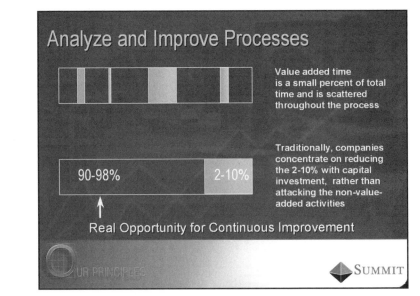

Figure 4.5. **Summit Second Agenda Item**

Figure 4.5 is the second agenda item. The top image is put in the lower left for future slides in this section.

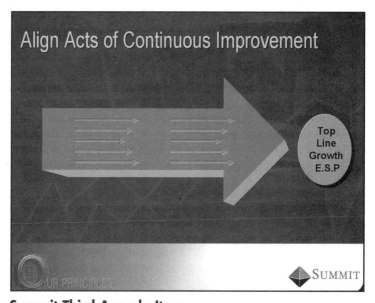

Figure 4.6.   **Summit Third Agenda Item**

Figure 4.6 is the third agenda item. Again, the image is put in the lower left throughout this section.

Figure 4.7.   **Question/Number Slide**

Figure 4.7 is an example of how to use numbers when putting questions on a slide. See first agenda icon in bottom left corner.

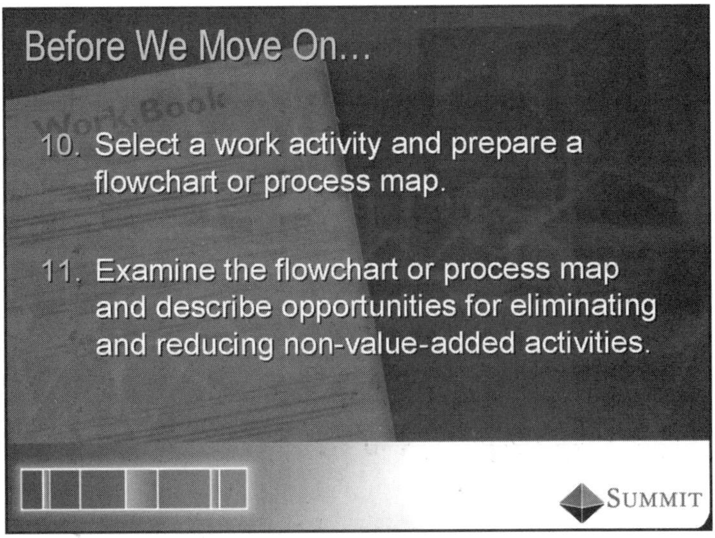

Figure 4.8.   **Workbook Slide**

Figure 4.8 shows a workbook in the background. The workbook image tells the audience to open their workbooks. See second agenda item in the bottom left corner.

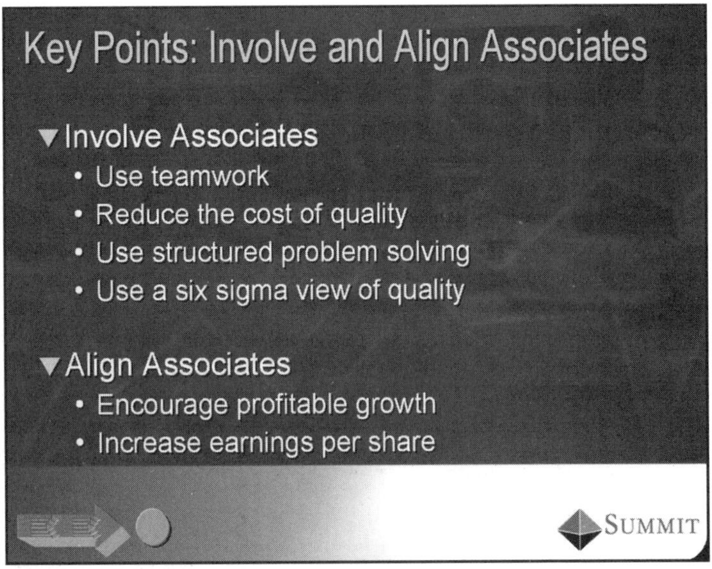

Figure 4.9.   **Two-Level Bullet Slide**

Figure 4.9 shows how to use the second level bullets. Also, see the third agenda item in the bottom left corner.

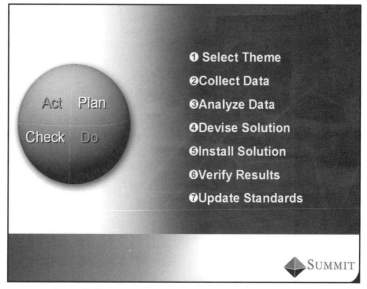

Figure 4.10. **Two-Color Slide**

Figure 4.10 is a new slide look. The right side is blue and the left side is white. This slide is for images with lists or words to describe the image.

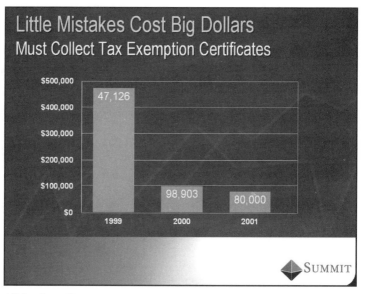

Figure 4.11. **Slide for Charts**

Figure 4.11 shows a slide for a chart look. The chart's colors are in the slide color scheme colors.

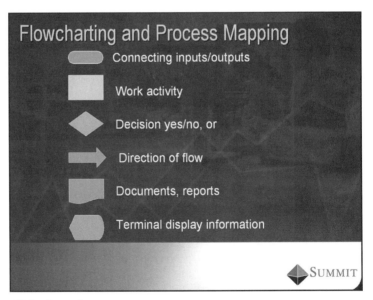

Figure 4.12. **Slide for Tables**

Figure 4.12 shows a slide for a table. The words in the table can be changed easily. Even the table boxes can be deleted if only three rows are needed.

Flowcharting and Process Mapping

Connecting inputs/outputs

Work activity

Decision yes/no, or

Direction of flow

Documents, reports

Terminal display information

Figure 4.13. **Slide for Diagrams**

Figure 4.13 shows a slide for a diagram. The colors on this slide's shapes match the slide color scheme. Using the slide color scheme gives the presentation the same look and feel throughout.

Company/Project Overview Example: The Nature Conservancy

The Nature Conservancy is the largest nonprofit conservation organization in the world. Working locally with businesses, communities, and individuals, The Conservancy has protected more than twelve million acres in the United States and has helped like-minded partner organizations to preserve more than eighty million acres in the Asian Pacific, Canada, the Caribbean, and Latin America. The Conservancy protects the land through directly buying it or helping to create long-term conservation strategies. The Conservancy's decentralized structure, with offices throughout the world, means that everyone really is "doing his or her own presentation creation."

But The Conservancy wanted to free up people's time in creating their slides so they could spend more time working on conservation issues. The organization also wanted to encourage presenters to help the audience connect emotionally with the places The Conservancy saves. Their work has always been based on the best available science. The thought has been that the science in the presentation would sway the audience to commitment. But that doesn't always happen. On the other side of the spectrum were the presentations consisting mostly of gorgeous photos. But showing an hour of gorgeous photos also doesn't convey a clear message. Neither of these approaches alone may motivate an audience to action. The goal is to inspire and emotionally grab the audience, then educate them. With respect to the slides, the prime objective was to have the audience connect emotionally to the places. Clearly, there needed to be a balance between pictures, science, and emotion. So here's what we did. First we began to look at the types of presentations most people gave. The formats we created include company overview and educational presentation.

Figures 4.14 through 4.31 show the corporate blueprint for The Nature Conservancy. These slides are in a file. The slides will be put into the different formats. Each format, overview, corporate, and educational, will have certain slide elements in it. Of course, the designer can use other looks as well, but the basic looks are already created with the appropriate color schemes. By having this structure set up, the presenter saves hours of time creating slides.

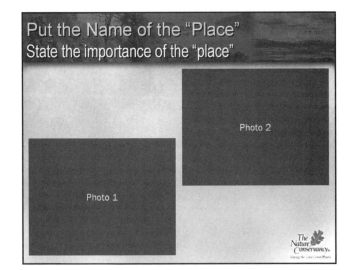

Figure 4.14. **Nature Conservancy Two-Photo Opening Slide**

Figure 4.14 shows a format for a two-photo opening slide. Photos of the place that is being discussed are shown on the slide. This slide can be on the screen when people walk into the room before the presentation has started.

Figure 4.15. **Nature Conservancy One-Photo Slide**

Figure 4.15 is a format for one photo and the agenda. This slide could also be an opening slide, the slide up on the screen when people enter the room, or a slide to be shown during the talk. There is a space at the bottom to put either the name of the place or other information. When the name of the place is put on the photo, there is a better chance that the audience members will remember it.

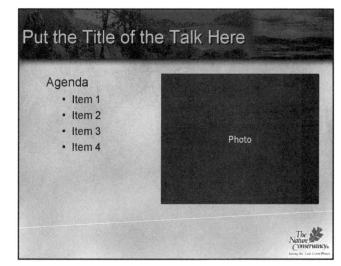

Figure 4.16.   **Nature Conservancy Agenda Slide**

Figure 4.16 is an agenda slide. A photo can be shown along with the agenda. There's no space for a long list of agenda items, which encourages a short, concise agenda. When the audience sees an agenda with ten points they inwardly groan, thinking they will have to sit through a lot of information.

Figure 4.17.   **Nature Conservancy Text Slide**

Figure 4.17 is a text slide. This slide has a place for a subheading. For example, if more than one place is being discussed, the place can be put in the subheading slot. Then when another place is discussed, that name can be put in the subheading slot. Project, country, and region names could also be put in the subheading slot.

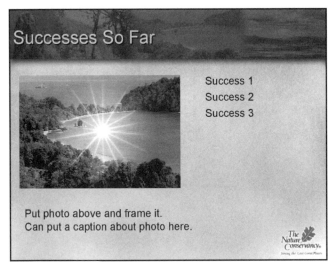

Figure 4.18. **Nature Conservancy Success Slide**

Figure 4.18 is a success slide. There's space for a photo and for the list of success items. This is a positive slide sharing what has already been accomplished at a specific place. The photo in Figure 4.18 was framed using one of CrystalGraphics PhotoActive FX I effects the Star Flare effect.

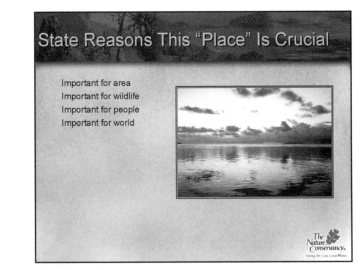

Figure 4.19. **Nature Conservancy Importance Slide**

Figure 4.19 shows an importance slide. This slide encourages the presenter to explain why the place is crucial in the world. On any of the slides with photo slots, the photo can be excluded so there is more room for text.

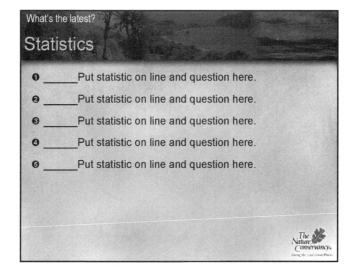

Figure 4.20.   **Nature Conservancy Statistics Slide**

Figure 4.20 is a statistics slide. Here statistics can be put in, along with the information. These statistics can wipe right after the audience has guessed what they might be.

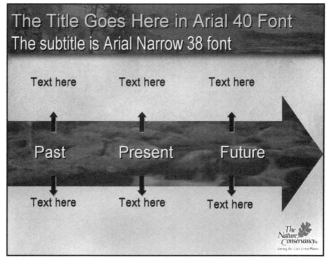

Figure 4.21.   **Nature Conservancy Timeline Slide**

Figure 4.21 shows a timeline slide. This is a different way to show information. The words Past, Present, and Future can be changed to places or countries.

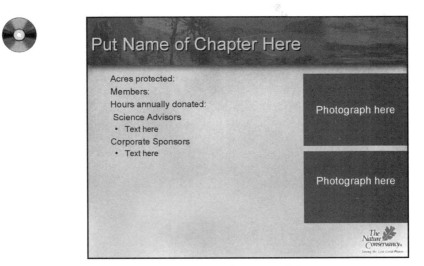

Figure 4.22. **Nature Conservancy Region-Specific Slide**

Figure 4.22 shows a state-specific slide. The presenter can discuss specific states or regions and their successes. The pictures on the left can be changed and statistics can easily be put in. The pictures are on the slide when it is shown. The numbers wipe down over the pictures. Finally, the key successes wipe right for a dramatic effect.

Figure 4.23. **Nature Conservancy Chapter Slide**

Figure 4.23 is a chapter slide. This is a design for chapters in The Conservancy, sharing how they are working to conserve special places.

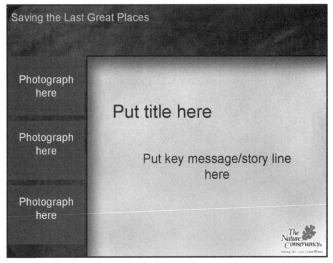

Figure 4.24.   **Nature Conservancy Section Slide**

Figure 4.24 is a sample of a section slide. This slide can be used to introduce a new place or also as an opening slide.

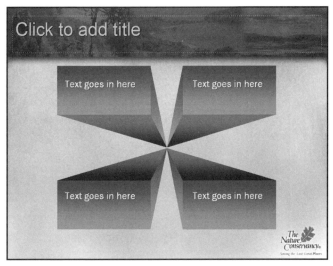

Figure 4.25.   **Nature Conservancy Shape Slide**

Figure 4.25 is a shape slide. Rather than use a text slide, the presenter can choose to use shapes to show information. Each text box zooms in on top of the shape.

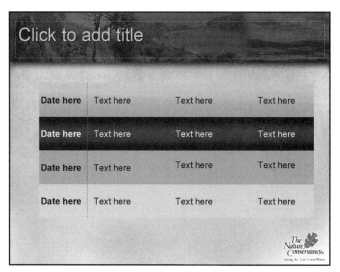

Figure 4.26. **Nature Conservancy Table Slide**

Figure 4.26 shows a sample table format. Sometimes information is best presented in a table. The rectangles with their text boxes can be deleted if not needed.

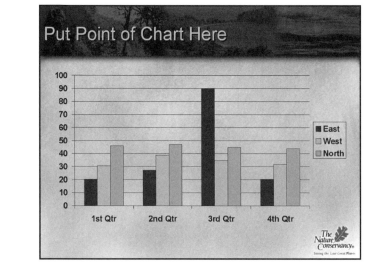

Figure 4.27. **Nature Conservancy Chart Slide**

Figure 4.27 is a chart slide, used to present information in chart form. Notice on the CD that the colors match the colors of the table and other images on the other slides.

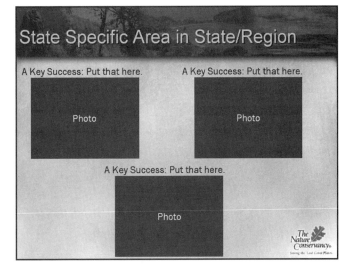

Figure 4.28. **Nature Conservancy Summary/Success Slide**

Figure 4.28 shows a summary success slide. Sometimes different projects and their success can be shown on the same slide, in which case the presenter would use this format.

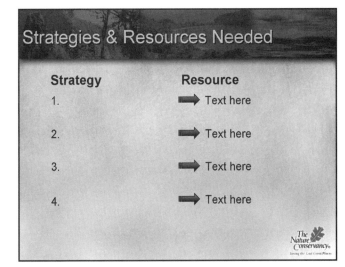

Figure 4.29. **Nature Conservancy Strategy/Resource Slide**

Figure 4.29 is a sample strategy/resource slide. The strategy is put in and then the resources needed are on the right. Each strategy and resource wipes right. This gives the presenter time to talk about each one.

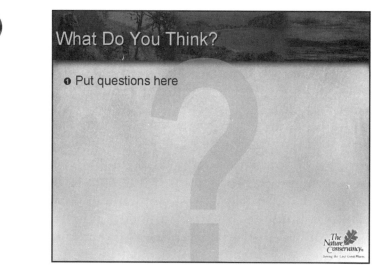

Figure 4.30. **Nature Conservancy Question/Interaction Slide**

Figure 4.30 shows a question/interaction slide. The presenter puts questions for the audience on this slide. It can be used at the opening to find out what they know about a special place. It can be used at the closing to ask them what they have already done to save special places. And it can be used during the talk to ask for suggestions in order to help save a special place.

Figure 4.31. **Nature Conservancy Next Steps Slide**

Figure 4.31 is a next steps slide. The number of steps can easily be changed, depending on how many next steps are required.

Selling Example: Harmon Inc.

Harmon, Inc., located in Minnesota, needed a presentation format for the sales force that would project the proper image of the company and still allow some flexibility for their distinct offices to customize their presentations according to the needs of the customer. To further complicate the issue, the presentations needed to be sophisticated enough to satisfy a seasoned Power-Point presenter and simple enough to use so as not to intimidate a novice. They also needed to appeal to a wide variety of customers with varying degrees of aesthetics—from no-nonsense building managers and general contractors to very aesthetically sensitive architects. In Figure 4.32 the photo in the middle will always be the picture of the project the presentation in discussing. So part of this slide will change depending on the project. Notice that there is a place for the name of the project at the bottom of each slide and that the name has as much prominence as Harmon's logo. Also see how the safety and quality control checklists have their own images. Figures 4.32 through 4.39 show the designs they use.

Figure 4.32.   **Harmon Opening Slide**
Figure 4.32 is an opening slide, on the screen when people enter the room.

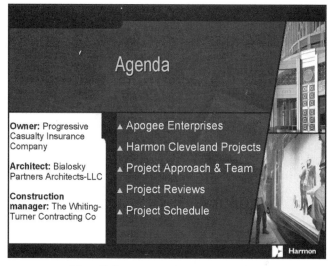

Figure 4.33.   **Harmon Title Slide**

Figure 4.33 is a title slide. This can be used as an agenda slide or a section title slide. There is also a place for the customer's logo.

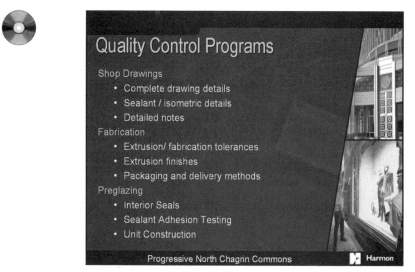

Figure 4.34.   **Harmon Text Slide**

Figure 4.34 is a text slide.

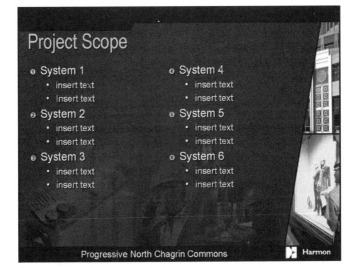

Figure 4.35.   **Harmon Two-Column Slide**

Figure 4.35 is a two-column slide. This is to show comparisons of products or just to have space for information. The slide shows "Project Scope" information. Harmon always has six project scope areas. They change the words underneath each area, depending on the client. A two-column slide is sometimes a more effective way to show information than just a text slide.

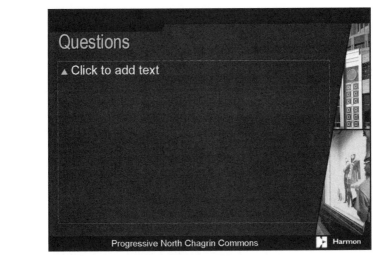

Figure 4.36.   **Harmon Question/Interaction Slide**

Figure 4.36 is a question/interaction slide. This slide reminds the presenter to ask the audience questions. The audience is encouraged to talk. This slide can come in the middle of the talk after the project scope, where questions serve to gauge audience reaction.

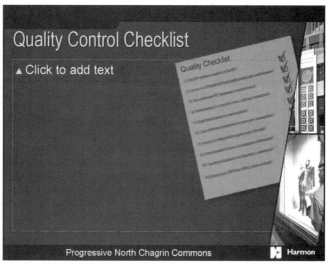

Figure 4.37. **Harmon Checklist Slide**

Figure 4.37 is a checklist slide. Here the presenter lists the quality controls they have in place. Notice project name at bottom of slide. Image is taken out on right. One image is enough.

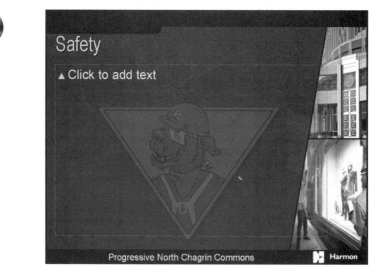

Figure 4.38. **Harmon Safety Standards Slide**

Figure 4.38 is a safety standards slide. In the background is a safety logo. When the audience sees this they know the slide is about safety information. Image is taken out on right. One image is enough.

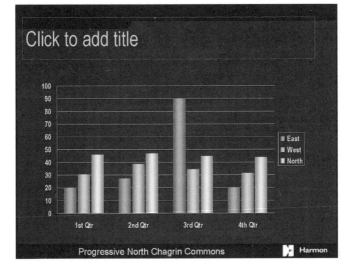

Figure 4.39. **Harmon Chart Slide**

The final example, Figure 4.39, is intended for charts. There are no images on the right.

Creating Backgrounds

Let's talk about how to choose or create an appropriate background for your situation. Here are four key guidelines to follow.

Make It Readable

What does this mean? Many backgrounds are so busy with swirling figures and pictures that text or charts put on top of the backgrounds are unreadable. A gorgeous design of swirling flower-like images might be excellent without any images on top of it. But when text and product photos were put on top, there was no focal point left on the slide. This very busy background might have made an excellent first slide or cover slide, but after that, the images needed to be put on the slide with clear space in the middle for the text and photos.

Make It Appropriate

All major presentation programs come with a variety of ready-made templates. The reality is that most of these should never be used in business. Consequently, presenters have to purchase business templates. Some of these are beautiful and very professional. Here are some key considerations in selecting a template design for business use.

Choose the Appropriate Corporate Image. What type of image do you want to project? Conservative, aggressive, or futuristic? For example, a plain blue background is a conservative image.

Choose the Appropriate Colors. You only have two choices: a light background or a dark background. Perhaps around the edges of the slide you can vary it, but in the center, where the text goes, you need either dark or light.

With a dark background you must use yellow or white letters so the audience can read them. With a light background you can use black, dark blue, green, or purple letters so the audience can read them. Don't use a background that starts light at the top and ends up dark at the bottom. Why? You then have to use dark letters at the top on the light background and then light letters on the bottom for the dark background. Now the slide looks inconsistent. Always ask yourself which colors have the best contrast, then use them.

Note that about ten percent of the male population and five percent of the female population is red/green color-blind, so they won't be able to see the difference between red and green on the screen. Red and green elements next to each other are indistinguishable to color-blind people.

You have fewer color choices than you think. Look at the color chart in your software program. Most of you will not be using the pinks, the light greens, the reds, or the browns in your presentation. Red is a warning color in many cultures so you don't want to use that as an accent color or as a background. When you take out those colors, you don't have that many choices.

Some people like black as a background color. It is very solemn. It is also not very interesting to look at for hour after hour. You want to keep your audience awake. On the other hand, a white background isn't that interesting either. If you use white so that you can show your charts and technical data, make the edges of the slide a color or design.

Colors Cause Emotional Responses. See Figure 4.40 for a chart on colors and emotions associated with them.

Know the Audience's Preferences. What type of audience will you have? Serious investors, participants in a training class, board members, company employees, customers? For example, if you are doing a two-day training class,

Color	Emotional Associations	Best Use
Blue	Peaceful, soothing, tranquil, cool, trusting	Used as a background (usually dark blue) in over 90 percent of business presentations; safe and conservative
White	Neutrality, innocence, purity, wisdom	Used as font color of choice in most business presentations with a dark background
Yellow	Warmth, brightness, good cheer, enthusiasm	Used in text bullets and subheadings with a dark background
Red	Loss of business, passion, danger, action, pain	Used to promote action or stimulate the audience; seldom used as a background; not appropriate for financial presentations, unless "in the red"
Green	Money, growth, assertion, prosperity, envy, relaxation	Used as a background color; good for presentations requiring feedback
Purple	Vitality, spirituality, whimsy, humor, distraction	Purple is impressive and spiritual and encourages vitality in darker shades; lighter shades can be detracting because they tend to be humorous

Figure 4.40. **Colors and Their Associated Emotional Reactions**

you may wish to have several backgrounds that look light and energizing. If you are speaking to board members, you may wish to cut the graphics down and just show the information they need to know. If you are talking to company employees, then you want to present the company image so that everyone can identify with it.

Identify the Presentation's Objective. What is your objective? To motivate, to update, to present good and bad news, to sell? A motivational speech will have a different background than a speech to cancer patients about their disease. A caring physician is not going to have a background with smiling faces and dancing figures when telling patients about their disease. A simple light-colored background is appropriate.

In this chapter you read how important it is to have a readable, appropriate background. And you saw that one background look is not enough. To enable the presenters and creators of presentations to save time and energy, companies need a set of background looks that they can use. Your first step is to choose the color and look of the first background, then to create other slides to go with that look. We guarantee you that your company's presentations will take on another level of professionalism if your corporate blueprint includes presentation formats and ten to twenty different slide designs. What's even more important, your presenters will be able to interact more effectively with the audience and deliver the message.

Blueprint Template Possibilities

A step-by-step process and a list of some typical slide design possibilities are provided on the Blueprint Checklist on the next page. First decide which designs are appropriate for your company presentations. Then look through the color samples of Figures 4.2 through 4.39 on the CD. Some of these design possibilities are in typical software programs, but the look and colors need to be modified. Seeing the slide designs in color will help you think about how you want your slides to look.

Blueprint Checklist

Yes **No**

____ ____ **1.** Look at the company's colors and images now portrayed in print and on the Web.

____ ____ **2.** Decide which of those images and colors will work well for slides.

____ ____ **3.** Look over three typical company presentations and choose the most typical slides that need a template look.

____ ____ **4.** Get agreement from the presenters that they could use certain slide looks in order to present the information more effectively.

____ ____ **5.** Create the templates and put them in a file that everyone can access.

____ ____ **6.** Do a short training on how to use the templates, being sure to show people how to work with the color scheme you've created.

(Continued)

Slide Options

Needed   **Not Needed**

_____   _____ *Opening slide:* This can be fancy, as it will be shown when people enter the room.

_____   _____ *Agenda/section slide:* If you don't put the agenda on the opening slide, then you'll need a slide for it. This slide can also serve as a divider for the different sections of the presentation if you wish to put divider slides in the speech.

_____   _____ *Text slide:* This is for text.

_____   _____ *Chart slide:* You'll need a slide that has a very simple background in which to display a chart.

_____   _____ *Photo and text slide:* This is where to show the product photo on one side and put text on the other.

_____   _____ *Table slide:* This is a comparison slide that can be used for product, project, and other comparisons.

_____   _____ *Two-box layout:* This slide can also be used to show comparisons side by side.

_____   _____ *Timeline slide:* This slide shows a timeline and can be used to show launch dates, a process, or project milestones.

_____   _____ *Question slide:* Questions can be put on this slide to ask the audience. Of course, in an effective presentation, the audience is interacting during the presentation, but this slide reminds presenters that the audience should be interacting with them.

Wonderful graphics and special effects. What do you think was the point?

Create High-Impact Slides

Now that you have decided the type of technology you plan to use, you can consider the design for your slides. For example, by using a remote mouse you can animate more images on your slides. If you don't have a remote, you don't want animations. If you carry your own LCD projector, you can use the watermark image, knowing that it shows up when you project it on the screen. If you have to depend on someone else's LCD projector, you may not want to create watermark images, as some projectors don't show them on the screen. You need to know your technology before you begin.

Slides are a key ingredient of any presentation. The role of slides, however, is one of the most misunderstood aspects of presentations. Slides are not intended to display the presenter's entire script, or even most of it. Slides are also not intended to display every specific issue. They should *highlight the key messages*. Word slides should not dominate the presentation. They should focus the eyes and minds of the audience on the main point while the presenter is speaking about it. Think of them as eye-catching billboard advertisements, not as full-page text ads.

There is a difference between creating slides and creating high-impact slides. Here's an example of what happens when you just create slides. A certain company's employees give talks on their products all around the world. They also train people inside other companies to give their seminar. They hired a graphic designer to produce the graphics for their presentations. The slides he created were gorgeous, but the show had one major problem. The graphics made it more difficult for the presenter to speak in a logical and systematic manner. The graphic designer did what he was asked to do—create graphics—but he was not the presenter. What looks pretty is not always easy to speak from. Animations and interesting images don't always make the speech any more understandable. The design may be stunning, but it is of little use if a speaker can't speak from it with style, enthusiasm, and clarity.

Four Elements of High-Impact Slides

The presentation lacked the four key elements for high-impact slides:

1. Emotionally engage the audience

2. Be understandable

3. Look aesthetically pleasing

4. Create a story waiting to be told

These four elements should be the core of every slide. Here's what they mean.

Engage the Audience. The slide must encourage the audience's participation—either out loud or in their minds. Unfortunately, after seeing the first five slides, many audiences wish they could leave. The slides should engage the audience's interest so that they want to hear the whole presentation. Most importantly, they should emotionally connect with the audience. Many people make decisions on emotion and then rationalize with the facts.

Be Understandable. The slide should, literally, be able to be understood in terms of its readability and its major point. Ever heard the saying, "Perception is everything"? Your graphics need to represent your message accurately and be designed so the audience is able to perceive the meaning.

Look Aesthetically Pleasing. So many slides break all the rules of design. In fact, many are quite awful to look at. A high-impact slide is appealing. One's senses come alive.

Create a Story Waiting to Be Told. Every presentation is a story. And every slide shares a piece of that story. When a slide is done well, the presenter can easily continue telling the story. Slides do that when they enable the presenter to speak with intelligence and add value to what the audience sees on the screen.

Applying the Four Elements

Creating high-impact slides is the foundation for a successful presentation. How do you start? First, you have to follow the three simple rules explained below.

1. Keep the Text Simple and Use Key Phrases

The most commonly made mistake is putting all of your information, in sentences, up on the slide, which makes the type very small in size. The audience is not motivated to look at such an uninviting slide, and you as a presenter are more apt to read the slide. Why do people make this mistake? Presenters feel nervous and deal with their anxiety by using the screen as a crutch. They put every possible issue on the screen. If you need a full script or many, many bullet points to jog your memory, by all means develop them. But don't put everything on the screen!

Keep the text simple by following these guidelines:

- Keep to one thought, concept, or idea per screen.

- Use phrases, not long sentences.

- Have no more than six lines and six words per line.

- Technical people or technical data presentations should have no more than eight lines and eight words per line.

- Use title case (capitalize the first letter of every word) for your titles.

- Use sentence case (capitalize only the first word in a line) for bulleted text.

- Use one—or at most two—readable, complimentary sans serif typefaces. Some examples of sans serif fonts are Arial, **Verdana**, and Century Gothic. We put their names in their fonts for you to see here.

- Highlight key words or phrases with bold or put in an autoshape.

- Highlight key numbers in charts.

Figures 5.1 and 5.2 show how text can be simplified. Both slides contain the same information. But in Figure 5.1, the eye gets tired of reading the slide,

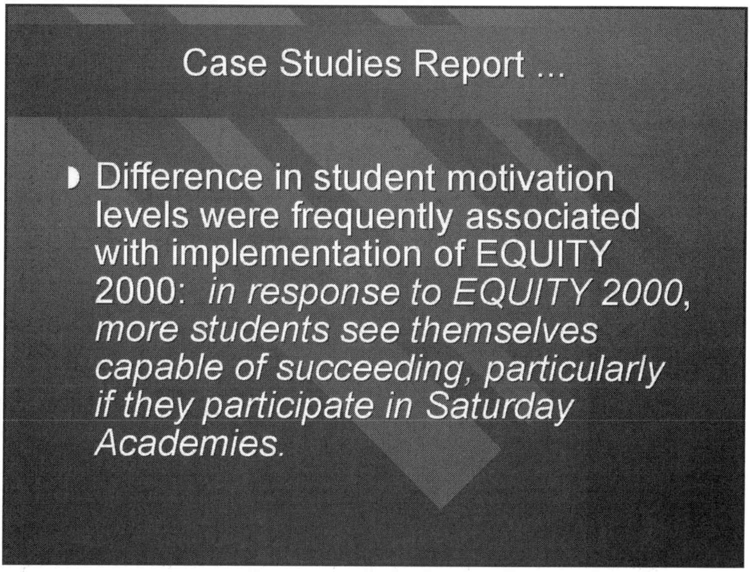

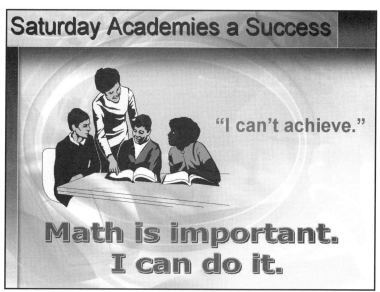

Case Studies Report ...

▶ Difference in student motivation levels were frequently associated with implementation of EQUITY 2000: *in response to EQUITY 2000, more students see themselves capable of succeeding, particularly if they participate in Saturday Academies.*

Figure 5.1.   **Before**

Saturday Academies a Success

"I can't achieve."

Math is important.
I can do it.

Figure 5.2.   **After**

while in Figure 5.2 the eye is guided through the slide as the text builds on the screen. This slide is a high-impact slide because it tells a story. The audience sees the picture of the children and thinks about how they felt when they couldn't do math. Then the audience learns that the Saturday Academies made a difference. The children began to feel competent in their math skills. Depending on how the speaker tells the story, the slide can also emotionally engage the audience in the lives of children who, over time, increase their self-esteem and competency in math. This example also shows how to take words and transform them into an image or picture. Most people absorb and process information more effectively when it is aesthetically conveyed. The creative challenge is to transform long text either into shorter text or into appropriate pictures.

2. Keep the Slide Clear and Spacious Looking

Ask, "What is the main point I want to convey on this slide?" Then only put information on that slide that relates to the main point. For instance, cluttering a slide with numbers is common in many business presentations. To get around this, ask yourself, "What are the key numbers my audience needs to be able to read?" Then design the slide around that key point. This approach will invite the audience into the message and help them grasp and retain the important point, rather than walk out with a cluttered impression of endless numbers and tables.

Keep the slide uncluttered by following these guidelines:

- Show only key numbers on a chart. If people need to see the trends and not the numbers, just show the trend line. But if your audience needs to see all the numbers in order to discuss them and reach a decision, then show all of them. If they are hard to read, give everyone a handout and discuss the numbers that way.

- Don't repeat the same word five times on a screen. Find a way to use it only once.

- Use graphic designs for variety. Use boxes of various shapes and put your key points in them.

- Have white space on the slides. Don't cover every inch of the screen with something.

- Keep images and text relevant to the slide's key point.

Figure 5.3 has lots of text and an image on it. First, there are too many different messages on the slide. Also, this organization is encouraging people to use their on-line service and the image is of a handyman. The quote is too long. Figure 5.4 portrays the same message in a better way: "Experts are on call for you." This slide is more aesthetically pleasing to look at; it is more understandable with only one message on it; and the presenter can animate the autoshapes one at a time and explain in more detail how the experts on call respond to requests.

3. Make the Slides Consistent

An often overlooked, but important consideration in designing slides is the need for the audience to absorb information in a short period of time.

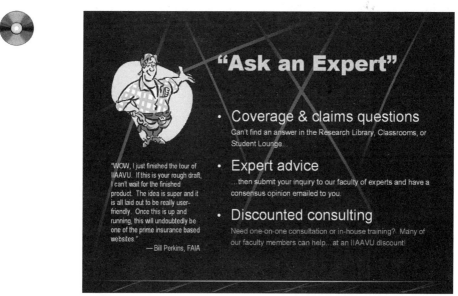

Figure 5.3.   **Before**

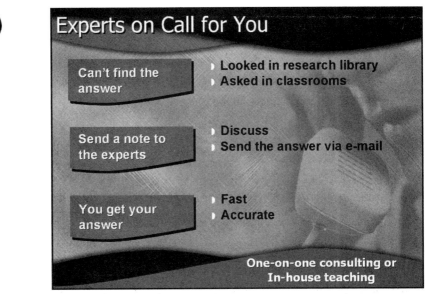

Figure 5.4.   **After**

By keeping the slides consistent in the way they present information, you will help the audience quickly understand the overview and the details. Figures 5.5 and 5.6 are an example of how to set up a consistent structure for a presentation. Figure 5.5 shows the five phases as a text slide. Figure 5.6 shows the five phase names as shapes. The slide is aesthetically pleasing and the phases are clear.

Figure 5.7 is an example of showing one phase. Every phase is discussed a bit differently. Figure 5.8 shows an explanation of the analysis phase. As each phase is being discussed, that phase's shape changes to yellow. The text that goes with that phase is divided into two chunks—the process to be done and the questions to ask. This creates consistency in the discussion of each phase. The audience can easily compare each phase now that each is explained in the same manner.

Further Considerations

Here are some other things to keep in mind as you design slides.

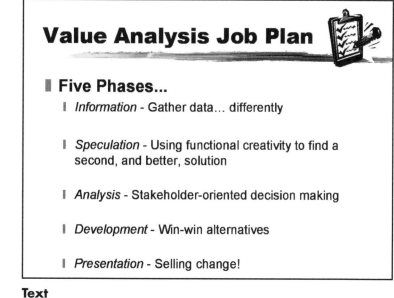

Figure 5.5. **Text**

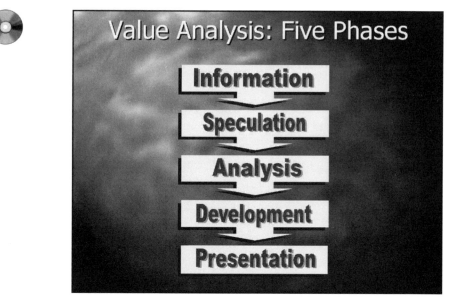

Figure 5.6. **Shapes**

Analysis Phase

▌ Keep the Stakeholder in mind. Do you *really*
understand their needs?

▌ Which solutions offer the best combination
of operational effectiveness, quality
and life-cycle savings?

▌ First identify and rank the criteria,
then rank the alternatives.

Figure 5.7.   **One Phase Only**

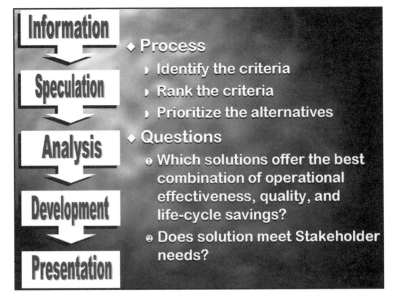

Figure 5.8.   **Outline of Phases and Explanation of One**

Covering Less Is Better. It is better to cover less information in a relaxed and energized style than it is to cover so much information that you feel hurried and out of time before you start. No one likes to listen to someone in a hurry who keeps saying, "I just don't have enough time."

Determining Length Takes Some Work. There used to be guidelines about how many slides to use in a presentation. Generally, you could plan on about three minutes per slide. Now in the world of electronic presentations it is different. When you use builds and show diagrams that are created in front of the audience's eyes, it is harder to judge how many screens you need for a thirty-minute speech. Practicing out loud is the only way to know how long it will take. (Speaking it in your mind won't give you a sense of how long it will take.) But for those of you who want some guidelines, here they are:

- Ten-minute speech: five slides

- Twenty-minute speech: ten to fifteen slides

- Forty-minute speech: twenty to thirty slides

The number is totally dependent on your subject and on how much time you plan to spend explaining each slide. A technical person could spend five to ten minutes on one slide. That's why you must practice out loud. Also, if you will take questions during your speech, create fewer slides. You may spend much of your time answering questions. Of course, you can show slides that clarify your responses.

Also, if you are a technical specialist and you tend to ramble, you should add some time for your rambling. Even better, learn to be concise and stick to the point, but budget in some time for detouring from the presentation's slide content. However, there is nothing wrong with not showing all of your slides. If your audience wants to discuss a different subject, then discuss it. If your audience is sold on your idea after the first slide, then stop. Your use of your slides should be determined by the audience's reaction, not by your belief that you must show and discuss every slide you have!

Learning the New Rules. More and more presentations are being given over the Web. Companies are seeing benefits in posting presentations for training purposes. There are some significant benefits. For instance, some presentations on the Web let viewers go through at their own pace. Web-based presentations also significantly reduce a company's travel expenses. There are also new and different technologies out there to help with the interactivity. These features include polling, giving tests, desktop sharing, and many more.

There are two types of Web-based presentations: interactive and self-paced. For interactive presentations, the presenter is there to guide the participants through, usually via a conference call. For this type of presentation, typical design rules generally still hold true. In the case of a self-paced presentation, you must take a different approach. When presentations are on the Web for viewing, people expect them to be more like Web pages—quick loading, lots of information, and easy navigation. As there is no presenter there to elaborate on the slides, short bulleted phrases may not be enough. You need to fill in the gaps in information, but be careful not to put too much on each slide.

Make the Best Use of Handouts. Think about what you want to give out as handouts and when you want to give them out. If you hand out your presentation slides ahead of time, you take away the element of surprise. Wherever possible, it is preferable to distribute handouts *after* the presentation. This keeps the audience's attention focused on you. But if they are the type of audience that likes to take notes about the slides, then give them the handouts before your speech.

Use a Reviewer. Ask someone to review your presentation, preferably someone who knows as much about the subject as your audience. You may hear suggestions that will enable you to create more effective slides.

Transitions, Builds, and Interactivity

In electronic presentations, transitions and builds can lead your audience from one slide to the next. They control the viewer's attention between messages. They also influence the pace of the presentation. The question you face is: "How do I use the transitions and builds to enhance the effectiveness of my presentation without overloading it with too many effects that distract my audience?"

The trend by software companies is clearly to offer users more and more transition and build options. These features can add value to the presentation so the audience leaves impressed and clear about the key points. Or they can create such a blur of special effects that the audience leaves agonized by the technology and confused about the key points. In short, just because the software company includes a certain feature does not mean it must be used in every presentation.

Some Guidelines for Transitions and Builds

Use the following guidelines as you design your presentation:

- Only animate certain pictures and diagrams, not every one. When deciding which ones to animate, ask yourself: "Will the animation of this picture or diagram contribute to the presenter more clearly and effectively communicating the slide's message?"

- Only use three different transition effects on the slides throughout the presentation. Having too many different transition effects distracts the audience.

- Use only two different slide transition effects between slides, but don't have slide transitions for every slide. It's just too much for most business presentations. Besides, you don't need to build every slide's information. Unless you have something of value to add, don't build.

- Change the pace. Don't do a build on every screen. Show some information all at once, so it doesn't get boring.

The Right Transition/Build Combinations

The selection of slide transitions and build effects provides a unique feel to a presentation—just as the color scheme does. For instance, imagine two presentations, one to a conservative group of bankers and another to a gathering of employees during their lunch hour (most of whom would rather be spending their lunch hour somewhere else). Does the presentation to the group of conservative investors call for a different tone, color scheme, and set of transitions and build effects than the training session on workplace safety during the lunch hour? Yes!

For the employee meeting, a lively box-out transition when changing agenda points, combined with certain text wiping right and pictures zooming in may help keep everyone's attention. These same effects may jar the conservative sensibilities of a financial audience.

The most common forms of transitions are wipes, box-in/out, dissolves, fades, and cuts. Here are some specifics for their use:

- Wipe right for text. Don't have the text fly in.

- Box outs and zooms are for photos and images.

- Peek from the top is excellent for showing a series of arrows flowing down the slide.

- Dissolve, fade through black, and zoom work well for slide transitions.

Transitions and builds are really movie-making techniques. Use them to enhance your story. All this being said, many, many people dislike seeing all the transition and build effects, so use them judiciously. One person said, "I'll go to a movie when I want to see lots of movie effects. Presentations are for sharing information. Just give me a few effects."

Navigating for More Interaction

One of the benefits of an electronic presentation is that, during the presentation, you can change the slide sequence. If you set up your slides in advance, you can easily go to another presentation file or to another slide in that file. Most presenters do not use hyperlinks because they don't know how to create them. Hyperlinks also require that you practice your presentation ahead of time so you can easily navigate them. Many software programs offer the ability to jump to any slide at any point in the presentation. The presenter types the number of a selected slide and presses Enter. To make use of this feature, print out a hard copy of your slides

Transitions and Animations

"I'd abolish 99 percent of transition and animation effects. As someone who worked on the product, I'm sorry that I ever helped put these things in there. There is almost nothing as annoying as sitting through twenty-three slides with every damned bullet flying in one at a time. My advice is to only use transition effects when they help communicate the information. Graphical builds that use arrows to move from one place to another are great. Flying bullets are the presentation equivalent of a light bulb on your tie clip—it's cool, for about three seconds. After that, it's just annoying. Using build slides repeatedly is a sign of what therapists refer to as 'control issues'; the presenter doesn't want the audience reading ahead. Well, if you, as a presenter, were interesting, they'd be listening to you, and you wouldn't have to worry about it."

—Cathy Belleville at www.bitbetter.com

(six to nine on a page) and number them. The following are some uses for hyperlinks:

- *Responding to questions.* In preparation for questions, create a set of "back pocket" slides (ones at the end of your file) to bring up on the screen when answering specific questions. You will leave an impression with the audience of a well-prepared presenter.

- *Skipping slides while presenting.* You may want to skip slides if the audience is getting restless or if you decide at the last minute to cut back on a topic.

- *Moving to products your audience wants to discuss.* Salespeople and technical specialists create presentations with hyperlinks so they can quickly move to the products that their customers are particularly interested in discussing. (See Figure 1.1, p. 11.)

Creating Hyperlinks

People's level of interest and retention is heightened when they are actively involved in a presentation, rather than just watching it. Interactivity can be an effective approach to creating such involvement.

A presentation can be designed in a number of ways to encourage audience interaction. The most common way is to set up a main menu with "hot buttons" next to each subject or with hyperlinks on the different subject areas. The presenter uses the main menu to trigger interaction with the audience, asking them to choose the subjects of interest.

Figure 5.9 is the "before" slide of Intellivoice's original main menu. They used a standard textured background from PowerPoint and only listed the topics to be discussed in the presentation. Figures 5.10 through 5.14 show how we customized and made this presentation interactive. This presentation is used by their salespeople to discuss the company's new concept. The presentation is divided into eight sections. When the salesperson begins, he or she can click on one of the topics and go directly to what interests the audience. On every slide is a "main" button in the bottom left corner that will take you back to the main menu page.

Figure 5.9.   **IntelliVoice "Before" Slide**

Intellivoice Agenda

- Company Overview
- VAD - The Product
- Automated Customer Name & Address (ACNA)
- Marketing Consulting
- VAD - The Opportunity
- Directory Assistance Call Completion (DACC)
- Orchestrate by Premiere
- Customer Service and Quality

Presentation to

Add Company Name Here

Add Your Name Here

main   Enter Date Here

Figure 5.10.   **IntelliVoice Custom Slide 1**

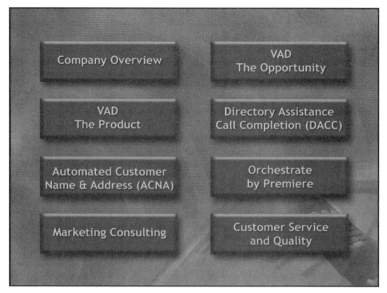

Figure 5.11. **IntelliVoice Custom Slide 2**

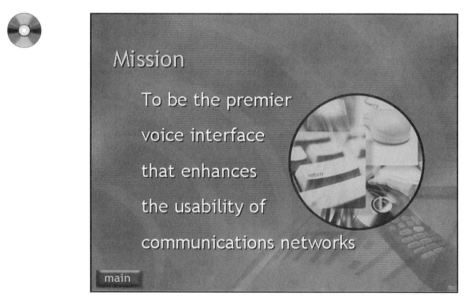

Figure 5.12. **IntelliVoice Custom Slide 3**

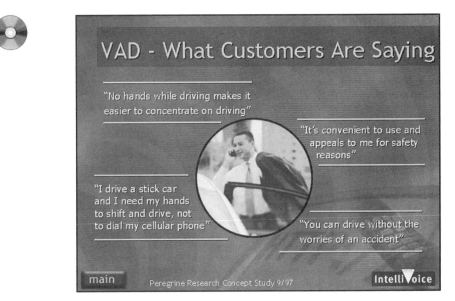

Figure 5.13.   **IntelliVoice Custom Slide 4**

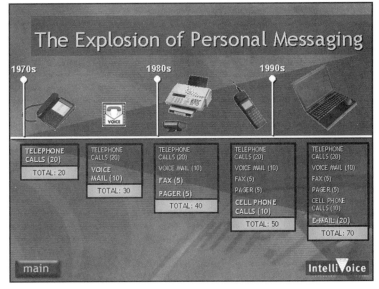

Figure 5.14.   **IntelliVoice Custom Slide 5**

Using Builds to Tell the Story

A major advantage of animations is telling a story. Figure 5.15 is a "before" slide from deliverEtoday, a company specializing in merchandise delivery. They have four bullet points detailing how their delivery process works. The "afters," Figures 5.16 through 5.19, show how we told this story graphically. The first slide, Figure 5.16, shows the U.S. map and then the targets dissolve in. These represent the delivery zones. In Figure 5.17, the map fades into the background and the clock appears. This represents the pickup times. In Figure 5.18, the clock also fades and a picture of their distribution center appears. This illustrates that after the pickup is made, the goods are taken to the distribution centers. Finally, in Figure 5.19, the distribution center fades and a house appears. The audience sees that from the center, the order is delivered to the customer's house that same evening.

The opportunities to use these types of creative builds are limited only by time and imagination. But keep in mind that five build charts in a row is too much. Intersperse them with other types of screens. Don't build every slide. In fact, don't even build every other slide.

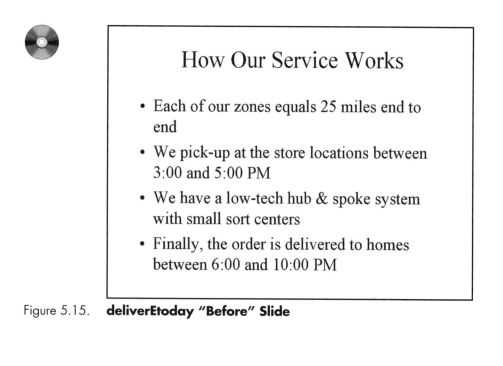

How Our Service Works

- Each of our zones equals 25 miles end to end
- We pick-up at the store locations between 3:00 and 5:00 PM
- We have a low-tech hub & spoke system with small sort centers
- Finally, the order is delivered to homes between 6:00 and 10:00 PM

Figure 5.15. **deliverEtoday "Before" Slide**

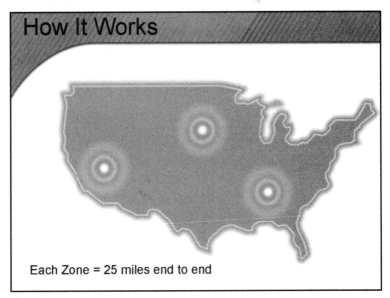

Figure 5.16.   **deliverEtoday Overall Map**

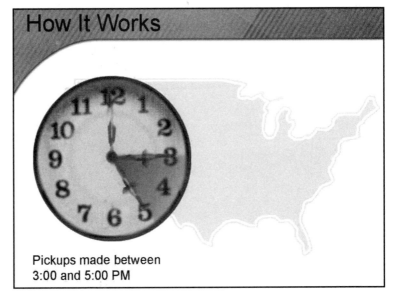

Figure 5.17.   **deliverEtoday Delivery Times**

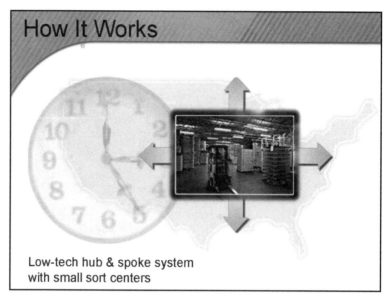

Low-tech hub & spoke system
with small sort centers

Figure 5.18.   **deliverEtoday Distribution Center**

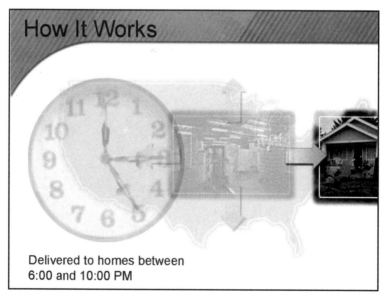

Delivered to homes between
6:00 and 10:00 PM

Figure 5.19.   **deliverEtoday Home Delivery**

Pictures, Clip Art, Charts, and Video Clips

Pictures, clip art, charts, and video clips add variety to a presentation and can make it easier to understand. Keep in mind that most people are visually oriented. They grasp information better through pictorial images. Also be aware, however, that extraneous or inappropriate pictures can get in the way of your message.

The first issue to consider is whether your computer can support the type of presentation you are making. If you won't be using your computer for the actual presentation, are you sure the computer you will be using is able to support all your fancy graphics?

Many people are creating their own pictures using a digital camera. They take pictures of the client's office or products. The cameras are fairly easy to use. If having certain client pictures in your presentation will make a difference, buy a camera and learn how to use it.

The following are some other questions to ask yourself when you are selecting pictures, photos, clip art, and video clips.

Why Am I Adding This Picture?

Some ways to get at the answer to this question include asking more specific questions, such as the following:

- Am I adding this picture, clip art, or video clip simply because I have access to it, or does it further my point?

- Is there anything in the picture that may offend or exclude part of my audience? Are there only men or only women in the pictures? Are the pictures only of a certain ethnicity? You must show variety in today's diverse workforce.

- Will the colors of the pictures look the same at the presentation location as they do on my laptop in my office?

- Will adding these pictures increase the size of the file beyond what will fit on one backup disk? If so, how do I plan to back up the file so I can have it with me in case I need it?

The examples in Figures 5.20 to 5.23 illustrate how pictures, when carefully selected, are more interesting than text.

Figure 5.20 is a typical "before" text slide. There are headings for the solutions, but the information could have been grouped on the page with more space between points. As it is now, it doesn't invite the eye to look at it and see these as four solutions. Figure 5.21 shows the same slide with a photo added. Now the solutions are easier to see and the slide is more inviting to look at and discuss. Also, some of the words have been deleted.

Figure 5.22 only uses words. It is hard to visualize the problem teeth. The picture on the "after" slide, Figure 5.23, makes the words on the page come alive.

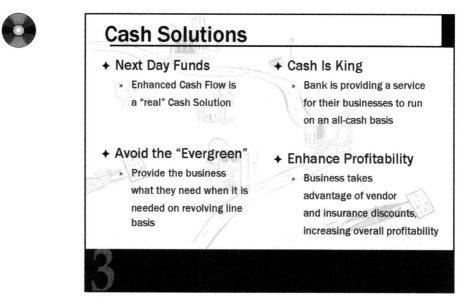

Figure 5.20. **Before Graphics**

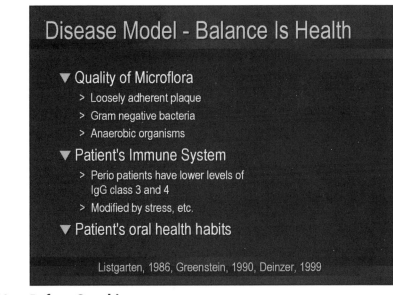

Figure 5.21. **After Graphics**

Figure 5.22. **Before Graphics**

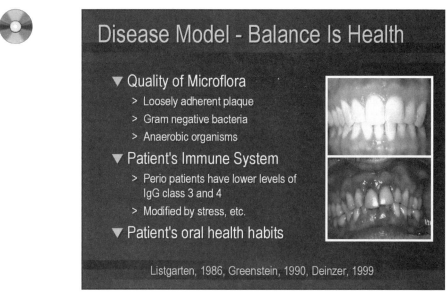

Figure 5.23. **After Graphics**

Am I Prepared to Explain and Comment on the Picture?

Have you ever suffered through a presentation in which the presenter showed many pictures one after the other, but never explained the point of each one? A picture may be worth a thousand words, but unless it is given context and meaning, it can be a different thousand words to everyone in the audience. Every picture needs to be accompanied by a title or phrase that makes the point and by an explanation from you.

Is Cartoon or Clip Art Appropriate?

Photographs, arrows, symbols, and diagrams, if they support the message, are appropriate for all audiences, from conservative bankers to company employees. The same is not true of clip art. Many clip art pictures resemble cartoons and, when included in a presentation, conjure up a tone and style that does not fit all situations. You be the first judge, then get a second opinion. This is especially true if you use the same clip art pictures that everyone else uses.

Is This Chart or Graph the Best Way to Make a Point?

Just because your software program will make a graph twelve lines across doesn't mean you should make one. Only use numbers if you truly believe your audience wants to see them. Sometimes a trend line is enough. After showing the trend line, you may want to bring onto the screen the key number that interests your audience. As we said earlier, colorblind people will not be able to differentiate between red bars and green bars. Here are some other considerations for your charts and graphs:

- Make thick lines if you are showing trends. We see many narrow lines that are almost invisible on the screen.

- Make the lines in bright colors, but not yellow. Yellow can only be seen on a dark background.

- Don't put more than five lines or sets of bars on one chart. It's frustrating as they may be too small to really see.

- Guide the eye to the main point of the chart with an arrow, a different color, a box, or by the heading title.

- Shorten all the numbers as much as possible. For example, put '01 instead of 2001.

- Use rounded numbers that are as short as possible. Instead of $10,400.34, show $10 (or $10.4 if the .4 is significant) and change the axis to thousands.

What Will the Audience Gain from Seeing the Video Clip?

Video clips can now be created using a digital camera. Just be sure that the video is of good quality. Here are ways video (and possibly sound) clips can be of genuine value:

- Video clips of company employees introduce them to customers or to other employees.

- Displays of products and manufacturing processes bring the products to life.

- Video clips of plant locations take the audience to places they may not have an opportunity to visit. They also show the audience that it is a real business.

- Customer or employee testimonials support your sales points.

Creative Slide Ideas

Looking at the way other people design slides often helps stir the creative juices. We include here a few particularly effective slide presentations to give you some ideas for your own.

Group Product Example 1: CMD Group

Figure 5.24 is a grouping of slides from CMD Group's sales presentation.

Features. The top slide is the agenda slide. Depending on the client's need, the presenter would click on any of the three boxes and move to the first slide in that section. Also, down the left of the slide are icons. These represent individual products within each of the three sections. Depending on which product is being described, that icon will be colored and the others will be the same color as the background.

The second slide is an example of how you can easily add simple elements to the background of title slides. The coin was added in the top right corner to signify that we are entering the Cost and Estimating Section of the presentation. This is the same image that is on the agenda slide.

The third slide is a creative way to show a comparison. Both the manufacturer and the building team have a lot of information to manage and the "information explosion" in the center represents this. Information specific to each group is then added to the boxes below their respective titles.

Helping the Presenter. Slide 1 makes it easy for any presenter to customize the speech. After the options are explained, the audience discusses their needs. Then the presenter can easily jump to the section that interests the audience.

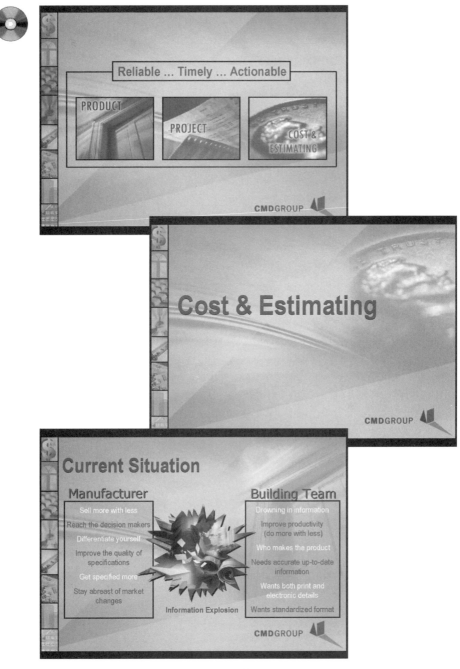

Figure 5.24. **CMD Group Slides Sample 1**

Group Product Example 2: CMD Group

CMD Group's sales force uses the representative slide presentation shown in Figure 5.25 to educate potential clients.

Features. The first slide of this set shows a unique, clean way to display information instead of using bullets. In the center is the main decision maker, and those in the outer ring are influencers. Additional factors that influence all of these individuals are displayed in boxes at the bottom.

In the second slide, the portfolio of products for this one section is shown. Under each product are some key bullet points. The icon in the top right corner goes to a mock Web page that gives more information about the products.

The third slide is an effective example of showing a product. There are main bullet points and then a shot of the product itself and the product being used via the Internet on the laptop screen.

Helping the Presenter. Slide one's simplicity enables the presenter to tell a story about the information. Slide two shows the pictures of the products all at once. Some people, visual types, need to see all the products on one slide. It helps them process the data. The presenter can then point out some of their important features. The third slide gives the presenter the flexibility to show the audience more information by clicking on the Internet button.

Custom Charts and Shapes Example: Transchannel

Figure 5.26 is a "before" text slide from the Transchannel presentation. See its after "after" version in the first slide in Figure 5.27. Figures 5.27 to 5.29 show how we used shapes and charts to custom design their presentation. These charts and shapes are designed to educate the audience on the application service provider (ASP) industry.

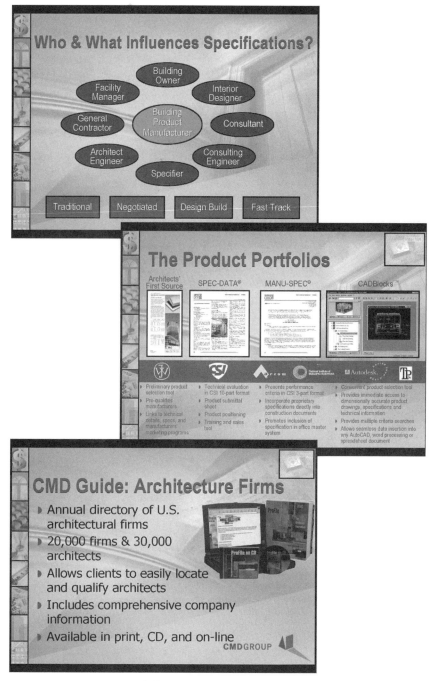

Figure 5.25. **CMD Group Slides Sample 2**

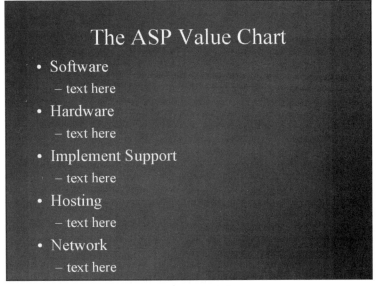

Figure 5.26. **Sample Transchannel "Before" Slide**

Features. The first slide in Figure 5.27 shows the natural progression of the chain. This slide also allows the sales force to enter their own bullets, depending on the needs of the clients.

The second slide in Figure 5.27 shows a pyramid image. Not only is the information in the pyramid discussed, but also the levels are segmented to show the different markets.

The third slide in Figure 5.27 shows the crossover of the vertical and horizontal markets.

Helping the Presenter. Slide one is customizable so the presenter can find out the client's needs prior to the presentation and then add them under the appropriate topic. Slide two allows the presenter to explain separately the top, middle, and small marketing opportunity segments. Each segment dissolves in. Slide three allows the presenter to transition into a discussion about the crossing of both vertical and horizontal markets. Here the presenter can also discuss how the client's market fits into this chart.

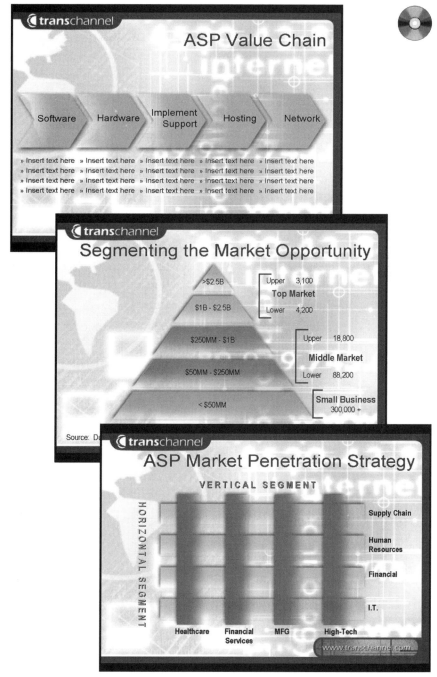

Figure 5.27. **Sample Transchannel Slide**

Using an Image to Tell a Story Example: Transchannel

A clear graphic can help explain a presentation's message. This entire presentation is built around the pyramid image. It starts from the bottom and builds up. On each slide there are bullet points that are specific to that piece of the pyramid.

Features.   Figure 5.28 is a list of bullets, not very interesting. Figure 5.29 is more creative. It shows the pyramid being built and helps the audience remember the point just discussed, PeopleSoft Applications.

Helping the Presenter.   This is a very easy speech to give. The image says it all. It builds from the bottom up, which allows the presenter to discuss the base, then move to the core and to the top-level information.

As you start to create your own unique images, shapes, and designs, be creative. Just be sure your creativity follows the specific guidelines in this chapter. Especially make sure your slides are aesthetically pleasing and understandable. Also find a way to have them emotionally engage the audience.

Ten Don'ts for Slides

Before you even fill out the Single-Slide and Total Visual Checklists at the end of this chapter, make sure your slides have not broken any of the following guidelines:

1. Don't use a gradient template with any type of image, for example, with an image of a building, when you are showing charts and graphs. It is very difficult, if not impossible, to read words and see charts superimposed over the images.

2. Don't make your whole presentation a series of builds.

3. Don't use so many colors that the presentation carries no consistency.

4. Don't use so many different models and diagrams that your audience never has an opportunity to fix one or two models in their minds.

5. Don't include so many words that you don't have anything to say besides what is written on the slides.

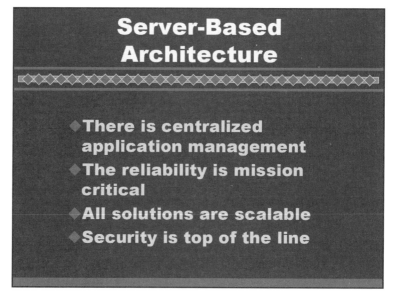

Figure 5.28.   **Transchannel "Before" Slide**

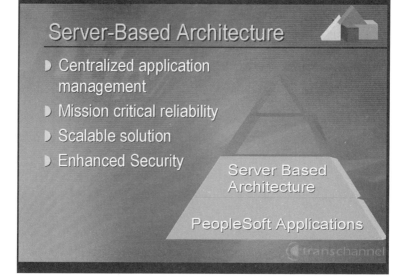

Figure 5.29.   **Transchannel "After" Slide**

6. Don't use photos that take up too much memory for the size of your computer. Your computer will take a long time to bring them up on the screen.

7. Don't use a black background.

8. Don't use sounds unless they are relevant to your topic.

9. Don't put so many numbers on a chart that your audience can't figure out the point of the chart.

10. Don't include so many slides that you know you will be short of time even before you start the presentation.

Some evaluative checklists are included to help you analyze your presentation and each slide. Print them out from the CD and use them for each of your presentations. Presenters tend to get too involved in the details of designing their slides. It is therefore important to sit back and look at the slides as a group.

So once you have created and analyzed all your slides, lay them out, one slide per page, hard copy, on a table and look at them. Yes, you can see them on the computer screen, but you can't see them all at once. Also, you don't get the same sense as when you lay them out and see how they all look together. Make sure the presentation slides follow the guidelines on the Total Visual Checklist to assess how well you have put together your presentation. Then, take a second look at each slide by making sure each slide follows the guidelines on the Single-Slide Checklist.

As you've seen in this chapter, a high-impact slide can enable you to present with more confidence and energy. Each slide can enable you to connect with your audience on an emotional level. It can give you a means to become a storyteller. And, most importantly, a high-impact slide can help you engage and connect to your audience. For in truth, that's what a presentation is all about—connecting with your audience and imparting your knowledge, emotional commitment, and enthusiasm so that they also believe in what you are offering, be it a product, a service, or an idea.

Single-Slide Checklist

Organization

Yes | **No**

___ | ___ **1.** There is only one major point covered on the slide.

___ | ___ **2.** The heading is different from the headings on the other visuals. (Different headings on each visual make them easier to present from and easier for the audience to grasp the main point of the slide.)

___ | ___ **3.** There is only the essential information on this slide; there is nothing else that I can leave out.

___ | ___ **4.** If text, consider illustrating the points with a chart, symbol, image, or picture.

___ | ___ **5.** There are no spelling errors. (Proof the slide by starting at the bottom of the screen and reading it backward from right to left.)

___ | ___ **6.** If there's a chart, the important numbers or images are pointed out.

___ | ___ **7.** The build helps tell the story and makes it easy for the presenter to talk.

Look

Yes | **No**

___ | ___ **8.** Photo is clear and doesn't take up too much memory.

___ | ___ **9.** The fonts are at least 24-point.

___ | ___ **10.** The colors used are from the slide color scheme.

Flow

Yes | **No**

___ | ___ **11.** The text is in phrases, not sentences.

___ | ___ **12.** The phrases are in parallel structure so they all start with nouns or verbs.

___ | ___ **13.** There are no periods after the phrases.

___ | ___ **14.** The animations are easy on the eyes. There is no flying text, etc.

Total Visual Checklist

Organization

Yes | **No**

____ | ____   **1.** There is a logical organization to the presentation that the audience will be able to follow.

____ | ____   **2.** There is an agenda slide and the presentation follows the agenda.

____ | ____   **3.** The content is organized with a format.

Content and Flow

Yes | **No**

____ | ____   **4.** Acronyms and abbreviations are spelled out for audience members not familiar with them.

____ | ____   **5.** Human interest examples are included through photos and images.

____ | ____   **6.** When seeing all the content, there is absolutely nothing else I can cut out in order to make my points.

____ | ____   **7.** Questions to ask my audience are put on some of the slides to break up the speech and to create more interaction with the audience.

____ | ____   **8.** The visuals don't all look the same. There aren't six pie charts in a row or six slides with heavy text in a row. (Have varied template looks throughout the slides.)

Look

Yes | **No**

____ | ____   **9.** The backgrounds on the slides have the same look and feel, following the template.

____ | ____   **10.** The titles are placed in the same location throughout most of the slides.

Look (*Continued*)

Yes **No**

_____ | _____ **11.** The photos and images go together well. (Try not to mix photos and clip art in the same presentation.)

_____ | _____ **12.** All the titles are done the same way. (Use Title Case where only the first letter in each word is capitalized.)

_____ | _____ **13.** The fonts and bullets are the same throughout so it looks like part of the same slide presentation.

_____ | _____ **14.** Some of the phrases are numbered for easier discussion of the information. (You can show a list and say, "Here are some key points. I will only talk about number four unless you want me to explain some of the other points.")

_____ | _____ **15.** The slides change in look (plot point concept), so the audience becomes more alert every so often.

Customization

Yes **No**

_____ | _____ **16.** Some slides are customized for my audience.

_____ | _____ **17.** Certain words are added based on my audience.

_____ | _____ **18.** The client's name, logo, and products are on my slides in different places.

Animations and Sounds

Yes **No**

_____ | _____ **19.** The slide transitions are easy on the eyes. There is no checkerboard across, etc.

_____ | _____ **20.** Sounds are used only if they are appropriate.

If I'd rehearsed properly, I would have known
to turn off the screen saver.

Rehearse, Rehearse, Rehearse

You must never kid yourself that you don't need to practice your presentation out loud using all your equipment and in the clothes you will be wearing. You may think you know how to use the technology. You may think you know where you will stand so you can see your laptop or the screen. You may think you can use that remote mouse you bought yesterday. But until you actually practice the speech, you don't really know how you will give it. The only way you can know is to practice in the same room with the same equipment you will be using. If you don't, you may be in for some surprises.

In this chapter we will speak about the types of rehearsals you need to do. We'll cover some of the technology issues that you should check on during your rehearsal and also provide you with a Location Checklist to be sure you cover all your presentation location needs. We include a real rehearsal flow chart for you to consider using, plus a Rehearsal Feedback Sheet for your audience to fill out. We include some thoughts about being in tune with your emotional state as you prepare and give a presentation. And finally, you'll receive some general refresher ideas on giving excellent presentations.

Do Two Rehearsals

Many people don't rehearse their speeches. They make excuses of why they don't by saying things like:

- "I don't have time."

- "I've been doing this for ages. I don't need to rehearse."

- "This isn't an important presentation. I won't bother to practice."

- "I'm too busy getting the information and proposal done to have time to rehearse."

Here's a scenario that happened to someone who didn't rehearse: "I once assisted a presenter who was using an untried computer to control his 'exclusive' new piece of computer software. Untried, without rehearsal, he first moved the computer and pulled out the AC power. The battery in the loaned machine was dead. When he rebooted there was no communication with the 'exclusive' piece of software. I spent the remainder of the time jogging from one side of the room to the other to press the right button to make the software do what it was supposed to do. Needless to say the product never really went to market."

In reality, the presentation of the material is as important as the material itself. This seems to be true more and more. So don't count on having the material and excellent slides make up for your poor delivery skills.

Do two rehearsals: a full dress rehearsal several days before your presentation and a mini-rehearsal just before your speech. Ideally, the full dress rehearsal is you giving the speech with the same equipment in the same size room with the same clothes you plan to wear. You can test everything out.

The mini-rehearsal happens when you arrive at the location to give your speech. You do a quick check of your equipment before you actually give the speech. You make sure your slides look good and the sound system works well. You make sure the power cord is actually plugged into a socket that works. In Chapter Three, go over the Technology Checklist and the Equipment Checklist. It is the strangest phenomenon how you can test your slides and they all hyperlink perfectly well the day before the speech and then, on the day of your speech, nothing seems to link where it is supposed to link. Better to know that before you start the speech than in the middle of it.

Now, what do you need to be practicing when you do your real rehearsal? We've provided a feedback rehearsal sheet to ask people to fill out as they watch you practice. Yes, have at least one colleague there to watch. Preferably, have one colleague who knows your subject and can point out any content inconsistencies or additions. Have another colleague who doesn't know your subject and can point out unclear points and transitions. Videotape your real rehearsal so you can see how you look. Most people are pleasantly surprised when they see themselves on tape. They say something like, "I look better than I thought I would." If you can't videotape yourself, you can audiotape yourself.

Here is a tip from Ellen Finkelstein, author of *PowerPoint 2000 Professional Results*. "When preparing for your presentation, it helps to hear what your presentation will sound like. One secret is to record narration for your entire presentation as if you were presenting. Then run your presentation and sit back and listen. You get an entirely different perspective when you pretend to be the audience. Listening to your presentation enables you to pick up awkward moments, unclear passages, and boring spots much more easily.

To record narration, follow these steps:

1. Attach a microphone to the proper connector on your computer.

2. Choose Slide Show > Record Narration and click OK.

3. Start narrating. Move through the slide show as you finish narration for each slide.

4. Click No so you don't save slide timings.

5. When you actually present, choose Slide Show > Set up Show and check Show Without Narration."

If you don't want to record yourself speaking, you can just practice your speech out loud using rehearsal timings. You can find out how long you speak about each slide and exactly how long the whole presentation takes to deliver. In PowerPoint, go to Slide Sorter and click on the Rehearse Timings icon. You will be in Slide Show. Practice your presentation out loud, then go back to Slide Sorter and see how long each slide took to present. When you actually present, choose Slide Show > Set up Show > Advance Slides Manually.

Looking and Sounding Professional

Here are the five keys to looking and sounding like a professional presenter:

1. *End your sentences and pause.* Have some silence between your thoughts. Don't always be speaking. When you practice this, you will eliminate the "uh's" in your speech.

2. *End each sentence looking at someone.* Don't end a sentence looking at the screen or your laptop or up toward the ceiling. End looking at someone. Linger a moment. Don't instantly dart your eyes away. Your audience will feel that you are really communicating when you look at each person. Your eyes give away your thoughts and feelings.

Speak to Each Person

Imagine that I am presenting to you. I want to convince you that my company provides personalized, customized, on-call service; but the whole time I speak, I look down at my note pad. In words I say, "People in our company answer the phone. You don't have to push six buttons only to discover you're on an automated line that no one will ever answer. We care about you." All that sounds great, but what feelings are my eyes delivering?

Presenters frequently spend half the time speaking to a slide, a note pad, or the ceiling. The spoken message of personal, excellent service is contradicted by the eyes, which aren't speaking to each person in the audience. Two contradictory messages are being sent.

It's not enough to make eye contact once in a while. You really need to speak to each person in your audience and end each sentence looking at someone. Do this for your next three presentations, or while speaking in a meeting, and notice the more favorable response you will get from the audience.

(When you videotape yourself, you may be shocked to discover that, if you don't look at each person, you won't really appear to be that interested in your audience. You will probably seem to be more interested in getting your speech over with and sitting down.)

3. *Hold your remote by your side and gesture with the other hand.* It is fine to gesture with both hands as one holds the remote, but don't just gesture with the hand holding the remote and keep the other hand by your side.

4. *Move deliberately.* Don't shuffle from foot to foot. If you want to move, then take two steps. There is nothing worse than watching a presenter who spends an hour shuffling from one foot to the other. Pick several spots in the room and walk to them. Just be sure that people can see you.

5. *Say more than is on the screen.* You must add value to the images and phrases on the screen. Tell the story about the slide. Emotionally engage the audience as you speak.

Do all of the above as you rehearse. If you must rehearse alone, pretend that you have an audience and that each audience member is being supportive and interested in your subject.

Using Notes During a Presentation

Here are some ideas for using notes if you have to use them during your speech. There is technology available for you to see your notes on your laptop and have your actual slides projected on the screen at the same time. But if you want to use paper notes, here are some ideas.

Imagine this. You had your slides all set for your presentation but wanted some extra notes to remind you of a particular point. You jotted your thoughts down on a piece of paper and planned to use those notes when you got to a certain point in your speech. When you came to that point, you looked at your notes but couldn't read them. Your handwriting was too small and somewhat illegible. Because you couldn't stop, find your glasses, read the notes, and then speak, you continued without them. BUT, at that point, you were a little flustered and upset with yourself. Maybe the audience noticed or maybe they didn't—but you felt uneasy for the rest of your speech.

Rule number one: Make sure any notes you plan to use when speaking in front of a group are readable. "Readable" means you are able to read the notes when standing with the paper on a desk in front of you. You can see each word with a quick downward glance. Print your notes; don't write them by hand. Use a twenty-four-point type size.

Now that your notes are literally readable, make sure they are concise and make sense to you. Don't use complete sentences. You just want some bullet points that remind you of what you want to say.

Rule number two: Do not write out your whole speech in speaker notes. You cannot possibly use those notes when presenting. Have as few extra notes as possible. You should spend most of your time connecting to your audience, not reading your notes. And always end your sentences looking at someone, not at your notes. Here's what you should put in your speaker notes:

- Opening sentence to make the slide's point

- Information you need in case you are asked certain questions

- Transition sentence to the next slide

If you write speaker notes for others, here are some ideas to include:

- *Speaker to do.* What the speaker can do at this point in the presentation, such as ask questions, show the products, etc.

- *Audience interaction.* How to involve the audience, for example, ask them to discuss in pairs the information just covered

- *Personalize.* What the presenter needs to add to customize the presentation to a specific audience

If you still feel you want some more presentation-type training, but have taken several presentation programs, take a theater course. There are many theater or improvisational movement/acting classes. You practice improvising on the stage. How can this help you when presenting? You learn to listen better to everyone because your next line depends on what was just said. You learn to enjoy the anticipation of not knowing what will come next. You may have had a plan for what was to happen next, but frequently had to give up that plan when the scene didn't go in that direction. You begin to appreciate your ability to flow with whatever is happening. Don't these all sound like skills you need as a presenter? Take a course. It will help you become a more relaxed, energetic presenter. Plus, you will have fun at the same time.

Plan with the Location

Be prepared. Based on our experience, everything goes wrong or fails to work at some stage in the life of a presenter. The best approach to dealing with all conceivable eventualities is to invest time up front in contingency planning and meticulous checking of details. One presenter has this to say: "I am careful, redundant, cautious. I have low expectations. I haven't had a 'fatality' in years." First, you need to work with the people who are setting up the room and in charge of the equipment. Don't just discuss the details with the conference organizer. Speak with the people in charge of the equipment. Frequently, the equipment requirements list doesn't make it to the actual people in charge of setting up the equipment. Speak to them yourself, if you can.

Confirm the date and time in writing. You may not think it is necessary. Here are several stories from people who didn't want to waste time confirming in writing. "I didn't confirm my presentation time and they had me speaking in the morning and I had it listed for the afternoon." "After much discussion, I thought we agreed on a day. No memos were sent. I had the wrong day on my calendar and was teaching elsewhere that day. Imagine my shock when I heard on my voice mail, 'Where are you? We expected you at 9 A.M.'"

You arrive at the hotel or company. You're about to set up your equipment. Are you ready? See the Location Checklist at the end of this chapter for details that you should have discussed before your arrival.

All of this preparation is part of your rehearsal. The more that you are involved in the setup and preparation, the more likely it is that you will feel in control and project confidence to your audience. If you have to use a podium, try to have it set up as shown in Figure 6.1. Here the speaker stands to the left of the screen at a 45-degree angle to the audience.

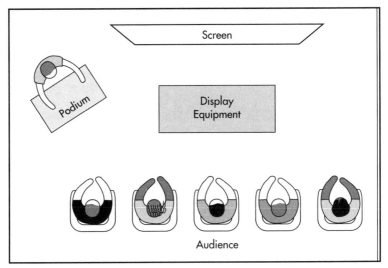

Figure 6.1.   **Podium Placement**

You've created an effective electronic presentation. To give it with style, go through all the steps shown in Figure 6.2, the Real Rehearsal Flow Chart. You owe yourself the time to practice.

Exhibit 6.1 provides a sample feedback sheet for your rehearsal. Use it as a guide for making one that you can hand out to people who serve as your "guinea pig" audience for rehearsing the complete presentation.

Work with the Technology

Rehearsals with technology are a bit more complicated. It is sometimes hard to find all the equipment in order to practice, but be persistent and ask people to set up a room with the equipment. You will be happy you had the opportunity to get a feel for all that goes into using the equipment. If someone else will be helping you, you need to practice working together to get your signals clear.

Here are some hints to help you present with style and confidence. We have gathered these ideas from numerous experienced electronic presenters.

- *Keep the arrow still on the screen.* Better yet, hide the arrow from the audience's view. Jim sometimes used the arrow to draw images on the screen.

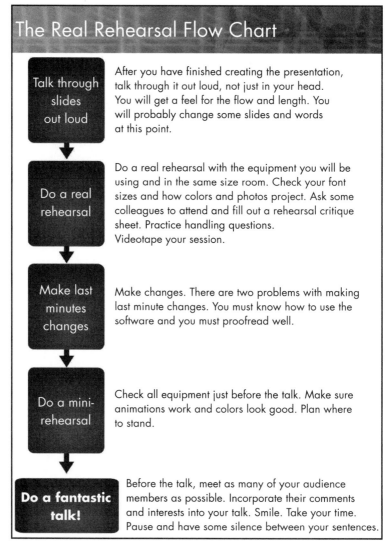

Figure 6.2. **The Real Rehearsal Flow Chart**

He was actually fairly good at the drawings, and his audience liked to see them. But after finishing the drawings, he inadvertently kept moving the arrow all over the screen. He needed to move the arrow off the screen when not using it.

- *Make sure the photos are clear on the screen and that the laptop you use has enough memory for your photos.* Michelle thought the photos looked great

Thank you for watching me practice my presentation. From your observations, please check or circle the items in the list below that you noticed during my presentation. Your candid answers will help me enhance my communication style.

NONVERBALS

☐ Standing in front of screen instead of beside it
☐ Shuffling notes
☐ Fidgeting with mouse or pointer
☐ Jiggling keys or coins in pocket

Eye contact	just right	too much	not enough
Movement	just right	too much	too little
Expressions	just right	overly done	too deadpan
Posture	just right	too stiff	too loose

Language

Technical words	just right	too many	too few
Examples	just right	too many	too few
Too many "uhs" or "ums"	yes	sometimes	no

Voice

Speed	just right	too fast	too slow
Sound	convincing tone	overly solicitous	unconvincing tone
Emotion	just right	too emotional	no emotion (monotone)

Technology

Spoke about words on screen and didn't just read them	yes	sometimes	no
Talked to the audience, not to screen or laptop screen	yes	sometimes	no
Used animation that helped explain points and tell the story	yes	sometimes	no
Held pointer still on screen	yes	sometimes	no

Please list two of my presentation habits or behaviors you see as effective.

1.

2.

Please list one suggestion for how I can use the technology more effectively.

Exhibit 6.1.   **Sample Rehearsal Critique**

on the laptop. How could they look so different on the big screen? Everything was washed out. She had never considered that the size of the screen would make a big difference in how the photos would look.

- *Use a fast enough computer.* The fades in and out looked great on the laptop, but the actual equipment that Bob used for the presentation couldn't handle the speed. The transitions were unbearably slow. Bob felt awkward and didn't know what to say during the slow transitions.

- *Make sure the expert is an expert.* Susan's company was told by the catering office of the four-star conference center that the center had people who ran the electronic equipment and not to worry. Her company had spent thousands of dollars putting together a presentation to be given to a group of consultants. Susan hoped to obtain a great deal of business by impressing the consultants with her expertise.

  Unfortunately, the so-called electronic "experts" at the conference center could not get the equipment to work. Susan never gave her wonderful presentation. Don't be fooled. The expert you speak to ahead of time may be on vacation the week you are at the conference center. Qualify the person as an expert, then find out whether he or she will be there the week you are using the facilities.

- *Know the environment.* If the meeting is at a site you don't control, the odds of something going wrong increase dramatically. Low-tech methods such as using overhead transparencies have fewer breakdowns. A financial consultant said, "If the site is my site and under my control, then I use the high-tech equipment. If the site is not my site, and not under my control, I go as low tech as I can get."

- *Be sure the site has the equipment you need.* Never believe it when representatives for a conference site say they have the equipment needed for you to give a multimedia presentation. They may have equipment, but not state-of-the art. Find out the brands, types, and capabilities of the equipment.

- *Practice with the pointer.* When you use a laser pointer, you must hold it still on one point on the screen. And you must leave it in one place long enough for your audience to focus their eyes on the spot you are pointing to. Follow these same guidelines when using the pointer from the software program remote mouse. Never wave it in your audience's eyes. People don't like that! Using a laser pointer takes practice—but not when you are in front of your audience. Practice using the pointer, and have someone watch you and tell you if you are using it effectively.

- *Check out the computer.* Check out the computer one last time just before the presentation. Then don't play with it, and don't let anyone else touch it. Don't leave the room with your computer on unless you put a sign on it that says, "Please don't touch the equipment. Thank you."

- *Work with your hired graphics expert.* When you hire a consultant to create a presentation, you need to direct him or her. You need to explain the type of audience who will be seeing the presentation, give him or her a sense of your business, and describe the levels of expertise of the people who will be giving the presentation. Don't assume the expert is thinking of all these things. We have heard of companies spending thousands of dollars to have a presentation designed, only to have to scrap it.

- *Be sure you can run the software.* When you hire someone to make a sophisticated presentation, you need to know how to use the graphics package it was created with. Why? What if something happens during the middle of your speech and you haven't the faintest idea what to do? You should at least learn the program basics.

- *Know the minimum requirements.* Save yourself the embarrassment and find out ahead of time whether the on-site equipment meets your requirements. Better yet, if you bring all your own equipment, you'll never have to worry about this issue.

- *Use the partner system.* For high-level key presentations, always go in twos. If something happens with the technology, one of you can speak to the audience while the other troubleshoots the equipment. A good pairing consists of the speaker and the expert on the technology. It's not a good idea to pair two speakers who are novices concerning the equipment or software program, or two technical experts who are inexperienced speakers.

- *Carry an extra bulb for the projection system.* One Polaroid dealer said, "The only bulb that always works is the one in your pocket."

The only way you'll know what could go wrong is to do the whole speech. This may expose many of the issues we just addressed, thus giving you an opportunity to correct what is wrong before it is too late.

Present with Total Confidence

You've now created a clear, easy-to-follow electronic presentation. If you want to give it with style, follow these simple guidelines. You've done your real rehearsal and had someone fill out the Rehearsal Critique Sheet. And you've planned how to incorporate their comments into your behavior. Here are your last guidelines.

Plan What to Wear

Practice in the actual clothing you will wear. You may have to climb up and down a platform, so don't wear anything too tight that won't let you take big steps. If you have gained or lost weight, be sure the clothes aren't so loose that they bag or so tight that seams will rip open or the zipper pop. (Not a pleasant experience when you are presenting in front of a hundred people!) Women, don't wear bracelets with loose jangling pieces, or every time you push the mouse button your jewelry will make a noise against the mouse. Now that every business has different dress standards, ask what type of clothing people wear. Don't assume that "business casual" dress means khakis and a knit shirt. You must ask, "Tell me, what specifically do people wear."

When people look at you, you want them to see your face. Wear something that highlights your face. Look at your complexion and wear a color that sets it off. For example, you wouldn't want to wear a light blue pair of pants and a black sweater. You'd do the opposite so the lighter color would lead them to your face.

Stand So You Can See Audience, Screen, and Notes

Plant your feet toward the audience. How you view your slide on the screen depends on how you have set up the room and the size of the screen. You can stand by the screen and use the slides on the screen as your prompt. You will probably not be standing by the screen if it is gigantic. You may not even be able to read from the screen effectively. In that case, you will need to see the images on your laptop. Consequently, you need to position your laptop so you can see the images. You may find that the table is too low for the laptop, so you will have to get a box to put the laptop on. You only find out these kinds of things when you practice out loud with all your equipment.

Control Your Inner Monologue

Some monologues that go on inside your head before you speak will not make you a better presenter. "I wish I didn't have to do this presentation. I don't know enough. I'll probably trip when I walk up front. I hate the way my voice sounds. I look terrible today. I just want to get it over with as fast as possible." Contrast that monologue with this one. "I feel great today. I practiced yesterday and feel confident. I look good. I'm ready to handle those difficult objections about my product. I can do this. I will enjoy each moment and not wish I wasn't giving the presentation. I want my audience to know I'm glad to be speaking to them."

Your inner monologue, positive or negative, sets the tone for your speech and sends messages to the audience. Which audience would you prefer to be in?

How do you begin to change a negative monologue? First, notice what you say to yourself now. Then begin to tell yourself positive, empowering thoughts. No one else can do this for you—you're the only one inside your head. When you change your monologue to a positive one, your body will feel relaxed and energized at the same time, your mind will be clear, and, most importantly, you will project a confidence that makes your audience glad to be there listening to you.

For a week before a presentation, just before you go to sleep every night, tell yourself three positive outcomes you expect from your presentation. Use the same outcomes every night—or select different ones. Here are a few ideas:

"I expect to have three new clients as a result of my presentation."

"I expect to sell the audience on my product."

"I expect upper management to agree to my proposed project."

"I expect to feel calm and confident while giving my presentation."

Handle Your Feelings

Before some presentations you may be nervous. In fact, for some of you, days before a presentation you may feel nervous. How do you not let your feelings take over? You have to let them out in a safe manner. Some people scream or sing in their cars. Some people beat pillows on their beds. Some people exercise to release their tensions. You need to have a method that works for you.

You also need to understand that sometimes your feelings will just be there. For example, a friend may have recently died. Someone you know may be very ill. You may be ill. Usually people manage to present, even if their feelings of sadness and grief are very raw and on the surface. What they don't do well is prepare for the speech. If you find yourself very upset, ask people to help you prepare for the speech effectively. You probably won't be able to do it by yourself.

A professional speaker was giving a speech at a company's annual meeting. He knew his subject. He had given the same type of speech many times. His father had just died a few months ago. He could not get motivated and organized enough to redo his slides and create new content for the speech. He just couldn't do it. And he didn't ask anyone for help. When he arrived to give the speech, about a half-hour before he was to speak, by sheer coincidence, someone started speaking about how her mother had just died. All of a sudden his heart was racing, tears almost came to his eyes, and he wondered how he would give his speech. He gave the speech, but he knew he was on auto-pilot and that he didn't connect to the audience in his usual manner. He also looked as his slides and realized he should have had someone redesign them. From that experience he promised himself that, from then on, he would pay attention to his emotional state and ask for help when he felt he could not prepare well by himself.

Be Quiet

Isn't that a very strange hint to give to a presenter who is supposed to speak? But remember that too much food, too much activity, or too much of almost anything overwhelms both you and the others around you. That's true with speaking as well. Everyone, the audience and the speaker, needs quiet.

The audience needs quiet time to digest your information. You need time to listen to the audience and sense their reaction to the speech. You also need quiet time that allows you to check in and find out: "How am I feeling? Am I heading in the right direction?" Both you and your audience need time to feel and listen to each other. If there is no quiet time between sentences and important points, the audience stops listening due to information overload. The speaker gets into the mode of, "I just want to get this over with."

If you really watch what goes on in many presentations, you'll see that no one is listening. If the audience members listened to themselves, they might stop the speaker to ask for clarification or ask him or her to go on to a topic of more interest to them. If speakers listened to the audience, they would know when to change the subject and how much to say about it.

For your next formal presentation, talk in a meeting, or even phone conversation, first listen and truly process the words you say. Second, listen for the feelings in the room. Then, speak based on your assessment of what your audience really wants and needs to hear. You will probably find you are more comfortable with the group when you actually present what you "sense" they are interested in hearing. Here's a list of ways to speak confidently.

Speak with Confidence

- Stand so everyone can see you.

- Ask, "Shall I say some more about this now?" If the audience says no, go on. Don't bore them.

- Ask, "Do I need to move back so you can see?" Don't ask, "Can everyone see?" They will be polite and say yes.

- Put the pointer down when you are not using it.

- If your hand shakes, get someone else to move the arrow on the screen.

- Say something else besides reading off the screens.

- Speak to the audience, not the visual.

- Write up and then ask some interactive questions to involve the audience.

- Practice the whole presentation out loud so you will know how long it is.

- Get a massage the day before your presentation so you will feel relaxed.

- Don't ask, "Can you hear me?" People will be polite and say yes. Ask, "Shall I speak a little louder?" Better yet, have a person in the audience cue you to let you know whether your voice volume is loud enough.

Practice to Get Better When Not Presenting

What has happened to practice? People attend presentation seminars and learn about some of their presenting issues. For example, they say, "I say 'um' too much," "I speak too fast," and "I get so nervous feeling everyone's eyes on me." The question for them is, "What are you doing on a daily basis to change that?"

Any presentation seminar is a jump-start to changing your behavior, but you have to work on change every day. You can't say "um" all day, speak too fast most of the time, or be uncomfortable speaking in a meeting—and expect those habits and feelings to disappear in front of a group. If only it were that easy. Instead, you need to practice every day.

For example, Terry is a high-energy personality, a little on the nervous side. She tends to get more like that when presenting. Her behavior won't magically change in front of a group. If anything, it will intensify if she doesn't know how to control it. So what does she do every day in order to be more prepared when she's presenting? First, she doesn't eat sugar—she has energy enough without it. Second, she meditates to calm her nervous system. And third, she exercises. Gradually, over time, she has become calmer and calmer in front of a group. That didn't happen because of a two-day seminar. The seminars and workshops she attended pointed out issues, but she had to practice every day. Here are some recommended strategies for certain types of problems:

- *"I say 'um' all the time."* Force yourself to organize your voice-mail message before you say anything on it. Listen to your messages and make yourself a deal that none of them will have "um" in them.

- *"I get nervous when people look at me."* Take your time in a crosswalk when a car is waiting for you to cross. Dress up and walk down a busy street where people will look at you. You'll begin to see that nothing bad happens just because people are looking at you.

- *"I'm scared to be or act stupid."* Go into a store and ask dumb questions. Notice that no matter how stupid you sound, the world doesn't cave in.

- *"I'm so rushed all the time."* Make yourself do one task at a time for an hour. For one hour speak more slowly, end your sentences, and pause for a moment.

These are all ideas you can use on a daily or weekly basis. Believe us, you will notice a tremendous difference in your next presentation once you begin to practice, on a daily basis, the skills you need to be a successful presenter.

Let's say you have done everything we suggest. You are totally prepared, and still something goes wrong. "What could go wrong?" you ask. The electricity in the hotel goes off. The company has a fire drill. Someone walks by and spills coffee all over your laptop. No matter what occurs, have a sense of humor. Get your audience to laugh with you. No one who laughs becomes or stays upset. Laughter gets everyone on your side. You can also remind yourself that whatever you're experiencing will make a great story in a few days. May you enjoy your fun, sophisticated presentations!

One Last Word

In the final analysis of a presentation's content and the presenter's style, what people appreciate the most is the presenter's authenticity. How much was the presenter actually in the room "being there" with the group? How much attention did the audience members feel the presenter actually paid to them? Some professional presenters break many of the rules we have suggested. They get away with it because they come across as passionate, full of energy, and totally engaged in their subject. Find ways to bring the best of you out when you speak. Some suggestions are listed below.

- *Know yourself versus your act.* You must know the difference between being "you" and just doing your "act"— "Joe the jokester" or "Mary the nice person." When you stop long enough to reflect, you'll begin to understand the difference. With some politicians it is easy to see. When asked a question, they don't answer it. Instead, they do "Act Number 20 on Education."

- *Take inventory.* Sit down and make a two-column list. Title the first column, "Times when I've been myself" and the second, "Times when I do my act." There's nothing intrinsically wrong with doing your act, but it may limit your ability to be spontaneous, connect with your audience, and discover new parts of yourself.

- *Take a risk.* In the next month do something that takes you out of your element. You'll be less able to fall into old behavior patterns.

The true joy of life lies in rediscovering over and over the delight of living in the moment. That only happens when you let go of trying to be, do, and act a certain way. Use the Rehearsal Checklist on page 191 to plan your presentations.

Location Checklist

Done   **Not Needed**

_____   _____   **1.** Confirm the date and time.

_____   _____   **2.** Type of LCD projector with specific resolution and if you need to hook up one computer or two computers to it. If two computers are used, they will need to give you a special plug. Ask if there will be a spare bulb available. Find out the brands they use and when they were purchased.

_____   _____   **3.** Table set up for the LCD projector and your laptop.

_____   _____   **4.** Screen size and placement. Ask: Will everyone be able to see the screen?

_____   _____   **5.** Podium: Where will it be placed and how tall is it? You want to be seen above the podium. Ask whether the podium's light will cast rays on the screen.

_____   _____   **6.** Microphone: Wireless microphone. You don't want to have to speak into a microphone at a podium. You probably aren't trained to do so, and also, people won't be able to really see you with the microphone in the way. You also want to be able to walk around and speak.

_____   _____   **7.** Lighting features: Be sure you can dim only the lights shining on the screen and keep the rest on.

_____   _____   **8.** Cords. Request that they be taped down.

(Continued)

Rehearse, Rehearse, Rehearse

Done	**Not Needed**	
_____	_____	**9.** Seating: You may have to move chairs around. If you have fifteen people and thirty chairs, the room will feel empty. Put the fifteen extra chairs off to the side. This is easy to do—time-consuming, but easy. I have yet to figure out what to do in a gigantic hall that is only half full at some of the conferences I attend and present at. Roping off a section of the room is one idea.
_____	_____	**10.** Room access: Find out what time you can get into the room to do your mini-rehearsal. Don't assume the room will be available when you want it.
_____	_____	**11.** Assistance: Find out if someone will be there to assist you in the set-up. If it's in a company, you may be on your own.
_____	_____	**12.** Restrooms and fire exits: Know their locations.

Rehearsal Checklist

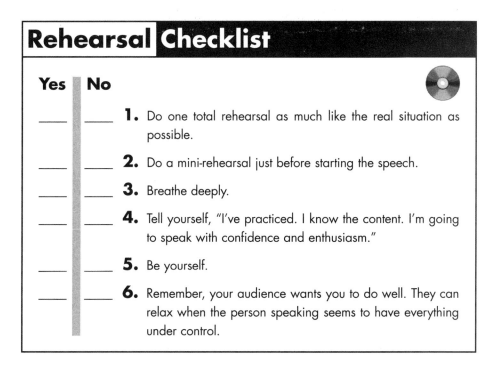

Yes   No

____ | ____ **1.** Do one total rehearsal as much like the real situation as possible.

____ | ____ **2.** Do a mini-rehearsal just before starting the speech.

____ | ____ **3.** Breathe deeply.

____ | ____ **4.** Tell yourself, "I've practiced. I know the content. I'm going to speak with confidence and enthusiasm."

____ | ____ **5.** Be yourself.

____ | ____ **6.** Remember, your audience wants you to do well. They can relax when the person speaking seems to have everything under control.

Resources

Wilder Presentations

Company

Your bottom line depends on your ability to sell yourself and your services. One way to achieve a competitive edge is by delivering powerful presentations. With Claudyne Wilder as your presentation partner, you will dramatically improve the development, design, and delivery of your presentations.

Services

Winning Presentations Seminar. This interactive seminar leads you through the three components of successful presentations—clear organization, effective visuals, and a persuasive delivery style. Special version for salespeople.

Individual Presentation Coaching. Personalize coaching for those who want immediate results in improving their presentation abilities.

Visual Makeover. A consultation on taking a specific presentation to the next level of organization, design, and pizzazz.

Speeches. Motivate your audience with a presentation topic of your choice.

Free E-mail Bulletin. A monthly e-mail with helpful hints on presentation techniques and technology. Sign up at www.wilderpresentations.com.

Products

CD. *Slides That Win: Your Roadmap to Success.* Compare and use over three hundred before-and-after slide examples done in PowerPoint.

Book. *The Presentations Kit: 10 Steps for Selling Your Ideas!* by Claudyne Wilder. See these ten steps at www.wilderpresentations.com.

Job Aid Card. Ten Formats and Tens Presentation Steps. Summary of *The Presentations Kit* book.

Presentations License. Receive all the presentation files and trainer's guidebook in order to teach The Winning Presentations Seminar.

Contact. www.wilderpresentations.com; e-mail: claudyne@wilderpresentations.com; phone: 617-524-7172; fax: 617-522-0617; Wilder Presentations, 57A Robinwood Avenue, Boston, MA 02103 U.S.A.

Creative Minds Inc.

Company

Creative Minds, Inc. helps you give effective world-class presentations. They specialize in custom PowerPoint solutions. They create effective, stunning PowerPoint presentations, as well as provide specialized software to enhance the functionality of PowerPoint.

Services

Custom-Designed PowerPoint Presentations. From corporate templates to road show presentations, they design a presentation that suits your needs.

Multimedia. Take your presentation to a whole new level by adding multi-media elements such as Macromedia Flash movies, or they can create an entire interactive piece for you.

Website Design. Keep your electronic media design consistent. They will take your current site (or create it from scratch) and redesign and structure it to a whole new level of professionalism.

Advanced PowerPoint Training. This training course is not for everyone! It teaches advanced features of PowerPoint that most people never knew existed. Plus, you learn tips and techniques from a seasoned pro, unlike what you will learn from a standard computer course.

Consulting. Not sure what to do with your presentation? Call them. A Microsoft Certified PowerPoint Expert is on hand to answer your burning questions and help you to evaluate your presentations.

Products

Slides That Win! This interactive CD ROM tutorial walks you through the ins and outs of great presentation design.

RunIt! This is a simple program to help you create presentations that "autorun" when they are burned onto CD ROM. There are two versions of this product, Basic and Plus.

Resources at Your Fingertips. The resources section of their website is packed full of tips and techniques on how to use PowerPoint successfully. Plus, they have their own "Ask the Expert" available to answer those burning questions. Visit www.CreativeMindsInc.com.

Contact. info@CreativeMindsInc.com or www.CreativeMindsInc.com; phone: 866-4-P-POINT.

Kayye Consulting, Inc.

Company

The company focus is AV technology and consulting, including specialized services to the ProAV (professional audiovisual) marketplace and consulting with corporations and individuals on their present and future AV needs. Works with corporations on integrating AV technology into a boardroom or training room.

Products

Sell the Margi Card. Lets you set up your laptop so you can see your speaker notes on the laptop and your slides on the screen.

Future of Technology. A one-hour keynote seminar that addresses not only AV technology but also focuses on the emergence of AV in the home and in the corporate environment and how AV tools can make communication more effective.

Contact: www.kayye.com; Kayye Consulting, Inc. 214 West Cameron Avenue, Suite C, Chapel Hill, NC 27516; phone: 919-969-7501; fax: 919-969-7561.

Brainshark

Company

The company helps others to archive presentations, with voice, on the Internet. You upload your files, give the presentation, and store the files for your audience to see and listen to on their own timing. Brainshark allows individuals the ability to create their own rich-media presentation. The presenter can store the presentation, with voice included, online. The presentation is sent to the Brainshark site. The presenter calls in and, over the phone, gives the presentation. Now there's a commentary that goes with each slide. Brainshark is made available on an annual license or a per presentation basis.

Benefits include:

- The file can be created at any time and any place for rapid communication

- As individual files are updated, the users automatically see the new version and the presenter can control whether or not the slides can be downloaded

- There is likely to be higher retention of the information

- A "guest book" can be added to determine how far the message is spreading

- Presentations can be edited and elements of one presentation can easily be integrated into another

- Access to the presentation can be managed and utilizations can be tracked

- Individuals on the road create presentations from their laptops. All they need is access to a phone, connectivity to the Internet, at 28.8 dial-up or faster, and a PowerPoint-Word-Excel document (no plug-ins or extra hardware). To listen, all they need is Microsoft Media Player/Real Player.

- Start-up time is about 30 minutes. Enterprise administration can be mastered after a two-hour training session.

Contact: www.brainshark.com; e-mail: ihipsman@brainshark.com or info@brainshark.com; phone: 781-313-3000

Echo 3

Company

Echo 3 is a presentation consulting and software development company that has developed a product called 3 Clicks Connect™ presentation manager

(3 Clicks), to make building and delivering presentations amazingly simple. This is important given that the responsibility for creation of presentation content is unclear and disorganized in most large corporations today. Back in the 1980s and early 1990s, only certain departments had the directive and ability to produce presentation content. With the release of PowerPoint and other presentation authoring tools, employees of corporations moved into a "self-service" mode of creating presentation content. While enabling employees to be self-sufficient sounds good, it has its share of drawbacks. A few of those are

- *Lost Productivity.* Employees are spending an exorbitant amount of time learning and "playing around with" presentation authoring tools such as PowerPoint.

- *Inconsistent Quality.* Because most employees are not trained graphic designers, the presentations they create and deliver are often lacking in quality and may not be brand-compliant.

- *Inaccurate Information.* Employees present the latest information they have on their hard drives. It is often out-of-date and/or inaccurate.

Product

3 Clicks. This is a presentation builder and media manager. It can be used by any presenter, but is ideal for salespeople. The software connects presenters across the organization to the all-important knowledge base surrounding a company's products and services. Using 3 Clicks, presenters synchronize their laptops to the centralized Media Library, search and find current and brand-compliant media, and then sequence the media to build a customized multimedia presentation. When a media element is either added to the Media Library or updated, all 3 Clicks users are immediately notified and can easiliy incorporate the updated and new media into their presentations.

Using their laptops, presenters simply drag and drop presentation media elements (slide shows, videos, executables etc.) into a staging area (called a Playlist), select a backdrop on which to display the media elements and deliver the presentation. 3 Clicks can be used in either a small group environment or in a large audience setting. The software comes with an interactive computer-based training course. The course and assessments take sixty to ninety minutes to complete.

Contact: David Kaz, president; e-mail: david@echo3newmedia.com; phone: 847-537-7400

CrystalGraphics

Company

CrystalGraphics brings you TV-style effects for your PowerPoint presentations!

Product

PowerPlugs. This is the leading family of plug-in products that bring the power and quality of television-style graphics and effects to Microsoft PowerPoint. *Presentations* magazine recognized this achievement by awarding CrystalGraphics with its annual Standing Ovation Award for "Best Power-Point Plugins." PowerPlugs product line of tools can add the following graphics and effects to your PowerPoint presentations.

- Incredible 3D transition and sound effects
- Visually stunning backgrounds
- Sophisticated 3D charts
- Animated 3D title slides
- Artistic slide headings
- Excellent concept photos
- Unique still and animated photo frames and effects
- Animated arrows and more
- Famous quotations
- Sophisticated template designs

Contact. www.crystalgraphics.com; phone: 408-496-6175 or 1-800-394-0700 in the contiguous United States.

Presentation Graphic Services and Products

www.NewEntrepreneur.com

Roger C. Parker is an author, consultant, and trainer who has delivered hundreds of presentations throughout the United States and Europe. Over one and a half million readers own copies of his twenty-five books, which have been translated into over thirty-seven languages. He has created and presented marketing and design presentations for clients such as Apple Computer, Bose, Hewlett-Packard, Microsoft, and Yamaha. His website contains dozens of helpful articles and worksheets.

www.bitbetter.com

This site sells screen beans clip art. Plus, they provide many PowerPoint hints and lots of other useful information.

www.ellenfinkelstein.com

Ellen is author of many presentation books, some of which are: *PowerPoint 2000 Professional Results, Flash 5 for Dummies,* and *AutoCAD 2000 Bible.* Her site offers tutorials, tips, articles, links, and her books.

www.bizpresenter.com

BizPresenter is a one-stop shop for your presentation design needs. They have thousands of professional photographs and illustrations. They also have a searchable PowerPoint tip section.

Presentation Websites

Presentations Magazine: www.presentations.com

A magazine geared toward all that presenters need to know, from audiovisual equipment updates to slide design ideas to delivery tips.

InfoComm.com: www.infocommnews.net

A source for presentation product vendors, audiovisual news, tools, and technology. There are sections on news, how-to's, and strategies for better presentations.

www.presentersuniversity.com

This is InFocus's presentation website with presentation articles and tips. They also sell LCD projectors and other types of presentation equipment.

www.presentationmaster.com

This site offers the latest product information, trends, news, and techniques for the presentation professional.

About the Authors

Claudyne Wilder is a communication strategist whose goal is to enable her clients to comfortably and effectively communicate with their prospects and customers. She works with companies to examine their communication presentation strategies. She evaluates every step of the presentation process—from crafting the message to evaluating the final presentation's effectiveness. Claudyne also provides individualized coaching so that her clients can learn to develop and organize content systematically, design audience-oriented slides, and captivate audiences from start to finish. Through her Winning Presentations Seminar and her Winning Presentations Sales Seminar, she teaches both companies and individuals the methods and techniques necessary to establish the rapport and trust that are necessary in today's competitive business environment.

Claudyne's Corporate Blueprinting Process enables companies to examine how to create more streamlined and audience-focused presentation strategies and processes. Her system of organizational formats (outlines) for specific types of presentations, combined with her methods of selecting appropriate slide designs, enables companies to accurately and convincingly reinforce their images and messages.

Whether one-on-one or in a group setting, Claudyne's unique combination of communication strategizing and coaching has resulted in many satisfied customers, including The College Board, The Nature Conservancy, Abbott Bioresearch, Mercury Computer, and The Gillette Company.

Jennifer Rotondo is the founder and president of Creative Minds, Inc., a presentation design company. She is a Microsoft certified PowerPoint Expert. She utilizes her abundance of knowledge in her Advanced PowerPoint Seminar and in several publications, including *PowerPoint 2000: Getting Professional Results; Understanding Computers;* and *Presentations* magazine.

Jennifer's company designs high-tech presentation tools for businesses. They take projects from start to finish, providing smart design and logical layout and helping businesses inform, persuade, and educate their audiences through high-impact presentations.

Index

Background(s): appropriate for business, 121–124; audience preferences for, 123–124; colors for, 122–123, 164; for corporate blueprints, 97–98, 121–124; creating, 121–124; creative ideas for, 156; guidelines for, 121–124; objective and 124; one versus varied, 96; readable, 121

Backups: CD, 63; for customer conference, 54; file size and, 84, 152; importance of, 81–82, 85; for international presentations, 80; laptop, 73, 76, 90; low-tech, 180; plans and options for, 63–65, 73, 90; preparing, 63; rehearsing with, 63

Bars, 155

Batteries: bringing, 65, 73, 82; charging, 72; checking, 65; cold cars and, 84; removing, to turn off the laptop, 84

Belcher, D., 180

Belleville, C., 143

Bells and whistles. *See* Effects

Birmingham, F., 100

BizPresenter, 200

Black background, 122–123, 164

Blank slide, 70

Blue, 122; emotional associations to, 123

Blueprint Checklist, 125–126

Blueprints. *See* Corporate blueprints

Board presentations, background selection for, 124

Body, 5

Borders, slide, 122, 123

Boxes, 134

Box-in/out, 142

Brainshark, 196–197

British spelling, 14

Browns, 122

Builds, 61; guidelines for using, 140–142, 143, 180; overuse of, 141, 143, 162, xxi; using, for telling a story, 148–150

Bulb, extra, 181

Bullet slide, two-level, 104

Bullets: animated, 61, xxi; number of, in international slides, 16; text of, 132

Business Week, 18

Busy backgrounds, 121–122

C

Cable connection, 62, 73, 88

Cached Internet pages, 81

Caldera, L., 21

Canned stories, 24

Car temperature, 84

Cartoon art, 154

Charts and chart slides: examples of, 105, 114, 121, 158, 160, 161; guidelines for, 126, 134, 155

Checklist slide example, 120

Checks: equipment, 65–69, 72–73, 82–85, 91, 171, 176, 177–178, 180–182; on language translation, 16; location and room, 71–72, 170, 176, 177, 189–190; rehearsal and, 176–177. *See also* Rehearsal

Clarity, 134–135

Clarity Advantage Company, 7, 25, 52

Clip art, 154, 200

Closed questions, 17

Closing lines, 48

Clothing: checking, 92; for customer conference, 54; guidelines for, 182

CMD Group, 156–157, 158, 159

Cold cars, 84

Colloquialisms, 15

Color blindness, 122, 155

Color(s): background, 122–123, 164; in charts and graphs, 155; checking projector's support of, 66; of clothing, 182; consistent, 162; emotional responses to, 123; graphics and, 151, 155; of logos, 12; of type, 122; using national, 14

Communication: data for, 20–24; levels of, 21–24; during presentation, 4–10; qualities for, 5; in sales presentation, 28–29

Communication Staircase, 21–24

CompactFlash cards, 64–65

Company/project overview example, 100, 107, 108–116

Comparison slide, 156, 157

Compatibility: checking, 82; in international presentations, 80; resolution, 67; software, 67

Compu Trace, 75–76

Computer, presentation. *See* Laptop computer

Computer Science Corporation, 26–27

telling, 24, 162

Employee presentations: background selection for, 124; special effects selection for, 142

Engagement: presenter behaviors that promote, 6–10; slide design and, 98, 131

Equipment: advance preparation of, 62–70, 86, 90–91; backup, 65, 73, 180; checking, 65–69, 72–73, 74, 82–85, 91, 171, 176, 177–178, 180–182; checklists for, 90–93; collecting, after presentation, 92; future developments in, 86–88; low-tech, 180; planning, 61–62; rehearsals with, 177–178, 180–182; setting up, 65, 66, 72–73, 74, 91–92; tips for presenting with, 70, 82–86. *See also* Technology

Equipment Checklist, 93; using, 171

Equipment investment presentation, 41–46

Executives, presentations to, 9

Experts: equipment, 180; graphics, 181

Eye contact, 77, 78, 172–174, 185

F

Face, presenter's, 182

Fades, 142, 148, 180

Fancy effects. *See* Effects

Feedback, rehearsal, 170, 171, 177, 179, 182

Feelings, handling presenter's, 184

File location, 73

File size, 81, 84, 86, 152, 164, 178, 180

File storage, 196–197

Film scripts, plot points in, 48

Film slides, 64

Finkelstein, E., 171–172, 200

Flags, national, 14

Flash cards, 64–65, 80

Flexibility, in presentation flow, 48

Flip chart, listing action items on, 30

Flow chart: of blueprinting process, 99; of rehearsal, 178

Flow chart slide, 47

Flow Checklist, 55

Flow, presentation, 46–48; for customer conferences, 51–54; dynamics of, 47–48; guidelines for, 51; plot points and, 48–51; for sales presentation, 46–47

Fluorescent lighting, 68

Follow-up dates, scheduling, 30

Font files backups, 63–64

Fonts, 132. *See also Type headings*

Formats, 41, 51; company customized, 97, 99, 107; for customer conferences, 53; examples of, 100–121; solution, 41–46; types of, 97. *See also* Background; Corporate blueprints; Slide design; Templates

Forty-minute speech, 139

Fraser, P., 28

Front row, 71

Full dress rehearsal, 171. *See also* Rehearsal

Fun, 26–27

Functional organization, 96–97

G

Games, 26–27

Gateway, 66

Gestures, 174

Gradient template, 162

Graphic elements, 134

Graphics: audience connection and, 18–20; checklists for, 164, 165–167; copyable, 84; do's and don'ts for, 18–20; examples of creative, 158, 160, 161, 162, 163; examples of slides with, versus text-only slides, 152–154; explaining, to audience, 154; guidelines for using, 151–156, 162, 164; resources for, 199–200; selection of, 151–156; using, to tell a story, 162, 163. *See also* Animations; Art; Builds; Charts; Effects; Photos; Transitions; Video clips

Graphs, 155. *See also* Charts

Green, 122; emotional associations to, 123

Group product presentation examples, 156–157, 158, 159

H

Hand trembling, 185

Handouts: as backups, 64; copying, 85–86; number of slides to print on, 40–41; table of contents for, 41; technical information in, 36, 40–41; use of, 140

Hard copies: as backups, 16, 64, 85; resource for printing, 201; for slide locator numbers, 70, 142, 144

Harmon, Inc., 117–121

Head nods, cultural differences in, 14, 15–16

Highlighting, 132

Honesty, 48

Microphone check, 91
Microphone, wireless, 62, 189
Micro-portables, 87
Middle East, 14
Military briefings, 21
Miller, N., 7, 25, 52
Mini-presentation, 70
Mini-rehearsal, 171. *See also* Rehearsal
Models and diagrams, 162
Monitor, reference, 78. *See also* Screens
Motivational speech, 17
Mouse, remote. *See* Remote mouse
Movement features, 61. *See also* Animations; Builds; Transitions
Movements, 174
Mutual fund company presentation, 39

N

Narration, recording, 171–172
The Nature Conservancy, 34, 35, 49; corporate blueprints of, 100, 107–116
Navigation, 142–144
Negative energy, 9; inner monologue and, 183–184
Nervousness, 4–5, 6, 132, 184; inner monologue and, 183–184; tips for, 185, 186–187
Networks: backups on, 64; integration of, with projectors, 87; presentation files on, 73, 85
Newspapers, as source of local information, 14
Next steps slide, example of, 116
"No," cultural differences in expressing, 14, 15–16
Nonprofit chapter slide, 112
Nonverbal cues, 10–11
Notebook computers. *See* Laptop computer
Notes page, technical details on, 36, 41
Notes, using, 174–176. *See also* Speaker notes
Number of slides, 139, 164
Numbers: graphic display of, 155; shortening or rounding, 155; showing only key, 134, 164. *See also* Data

O

Objective: background look and, 124; examples of, 40; organizing around, 34–56; questions answered by, 34, 36; sales versus technical, 36, 39; setting, 36–41

Offensiveness: cultural differences in, 15; in graphics, 151; in laptop content, 78–79
One-person presentation, 79
Opening lines, 46, 48, 175
Opening slides: examples of, 28, 101, 108, 117; guidelines for, 125
Organization, 34–56; for audience connection, 20; of customer conferences, 51–54; formats for, 41; of international presentations, 16; plot-point theory of, 48–51; presentation flow and, 46–48; presentation objective and, 34–41; solution format for, 41–46. *See also* Corporate blueprints
Outline slides, 10; sample, 11; types of, 97
Overheads: as backups, 81–82, 180; role of presenters and, 5
Overview slide, sample format for, 107
Overwritten files, 82

P

Pace, 141
Paper notes, 174–176. *See also* Speaker notes
Parallel phrases, 16
Parker, R. C., 64, 199–200
Partners or assistants: assigning tasks to, 92; with backups, 64; for customer conference presentations, 54; using, 181
Passion, 6, 8
PC CARD slot, 65
PCMCIA slot, 65
PDF files, 64, 81
Performance presenters, 17
Personal stories, 24
Persuasion, titles for, 40
Phases, showing, with consistency, 136, 137, 138
Photo slides: example of, 108; guidelines for, 126
Photos: for audience customization, 13; guidelines for, 151–156, 164, 178, 180. *See also* Graphics
Phrases: engaging versus nonengaging, 6; for international presentations, 16; using key, 132
Pictures, 151–156. *See also* Graphics
Pink, 122
Plant location, video clips of, 156
Player, 65
Plot Point One, 48, 49

Technology Checklist, 90–92; using, 171

Technology, presentation, 60–93; advance preparation of, 62–70; future of, 86–88, 139–140; general issues of, 61–62; for international presentations, 80–81; lightweight, 89; matching, to the message and presenter, 70; need for familiarity with, 60, 62, 181; overuse of, 141, xx; rehearsals with, 177–178, 180–182; setup of, 72–73; slide design and, 130; tips for presenting with, 70; Web, 139–140; worst scenarios in, 63. *See also* Equipment

Telephone line connection, 83

Templates: for audience appeal, 19; business, selection of, 122–124; for customer conference, 53; gradient, 162; packaged with presentation software, 121–122. *See also* Corporate blueprints; Formats

Ten-minute speech, 139

Texas Instruments, 87

Texas Legislature, presentation to, 22–24

Text: amount of, 132, 162; guidelines for, 132–134; in international presentations, 16

Text slides: design of, 132–134; examples of, 101, 109, 118; graphic slides versus, 152–154

Theft, of laptops, 74–75; protecting against, 75–76

3 Clicks Connect, 197–198

3D, 61

Three-person audience, equipment for, 62

Time of presentation: confirmation of, 176; to enable a run-through, 82–83, 91; factors in, 9. *See also* Length of presentation

Time savings, of corporate blueprints, 98

Timeline slides: example of, 111; guidelines for, 126

Timer, 68

Timings, rehearsing, 172

Title slides, examples of, 118, 156, 157

Titles, slide: to persuade, 40; typeface for, 132

Total Visual Checklist, 166–167; using, 53, 164

Tours, multiple country, 16

Training: for customer conference slide design, 53; in improvisational theater, 175–176; in presentation technology, 60, 62, 96, 181; 195

Training presentation example, 100, 101–106

Transchannel, 158, 160, 161, 162, 163

Transitions, 61; checking, 64, 180; forms of, 142; guidelines for using, 140–142, 143; number of, to use, 141; overuse of, 141, 143, xxi; video drivers and, 64

Translation issues, 15, 16, 80

Transparencies, 64. *See also* Overheads

Trembling, 185

Trend line, 134, 155

Tripping, over cords, 72

Twenty-minute speech, 139

Two-box layout, 126

Two-color slide, 105

Two-column slide, 119

Type color, 122

Type size: amount of text and, 132; screen size and, 66; small, 81, 132

Typefaces, 132

U

"Um," 186

Understandability, of slides, 131

Union of Concerned Scientists (UCS), 49, 50, 51

V

Variety: in background, 96; in effects, 141; in graphics, 49; plot points and, 48–51; in speech, 49

VESTAR, 28

Video clips, 61; backup copy of, 63; guidelines for, 151–152, 155–156; uses of, 155–156

Video settings and drivers, 64; checking, 66–67

Videotaping, of rehearsal, 171, 174

Visuals. *See* Effects; Graphics

Voice, 5, 6, 8; volume of, 186

W

Wall Street Journal, *21*

Water, 74, 92

Watermarked slides: technological considerations in, 130; testing, 66

Weaver, B., 181

Web-based presentations, 139–140, 196–197

Websites, presentation, 200–201. *See also* Resources

White: background, 123, xxi; emotional associations to, 123
White space: for logo, 100; in slide design, 135
Whiteboards, 84
"Who Wants to Be a Millionaire?", 26–27
Wilder, C., 41, 48, 193–194
Wilder Presentations, 192, 193–194
Windows NT, 72
Wipes, 142
Wireless microphone, 62, 189
Wireless radio frequency (RF) mouse, 68

Words per line, 132
Workbook slide example, 104
"Wow," meaning of, 4

Y

Yellow, 122, 155; emotional associations to, 123
"Yes," cultural differences in expressing, 14, 15–16

Z

zTrace, 76

How to Use the CD-ROM

System Requirements

Windows PC

- 486 or Pentium processor-based personal computer
- Microsoft Windows 95 or Windows NT 3.51 or later
- Minimum RAM: 8 MB for Windows 95 and NT
- Available space on hard disk: 8 MB Windows 95 and NT
- 2X speed CD-ROM drive or faster

Netscape 3.0 or higher browser or MS Internet Explorer 3.0 or higher

Macintosh

- Macintosh with a 68020 or higher processor or Power Macintosh
- Apple OS version 7.0 or later
- Minimum RAM: 12 MB for Macintosh
- Available space on hard disk: 6 MB Macintosh
- 2X speed CD-ROM drive or faster

Netscape 3.0 or higher browser or MS Internet Explorer 3.0 or higher

NOTE: This CD requires Netscape 3.0 or MS Internet Explorer 3.0 or higher. You can download these products using the links on the CD-ROM Help Page.

Getting Started

Insert the CD-ROM into your drive. The CD-ROM will usually launch automatically. If it does not, click on the CD-ROM drive on your computer to launch. You will see an opening page. You can click on this page or wait for it to fade to the Copyright Page. After you click to agree to the terms of the Copyright Page, the Home Page will appear.

Moving Around

Use the buttons at the left of each screen or the underlined text at the bottom of each screen to move among the menu pages. To view a document listed on one of the menu pages, simply click on the name of the document. To quit a document at any time, click the box at the upper right-hand corner of the screen.

Use the scrollbar at the right of the screen to scroll up and down each page.

To quit the CD-ROM, you can click the Quit option at the bottom of each menu page, hit Control-Q, or click the box at the upper right-hand corner of the screen.

To Download Documents

Open the document you wish to download. Under the File pulldown menu, choose Save As. Save the document onto your hard drive with a different name. It is important to use a different name, otherwise the document may remain a read-only file.

You can also click on your CD drive in Windows Explorer and select a document to copy it to your hard drive and rename it.

In Case of Trouble

If you experience difficulty using the *Point, Click & Wow!* CD-ROM, please follow these steps:

1. Make sure your hardware and systems configurations conform to the systems requirements noted under "Systems Requirements" above.

2. Review the installation procedure for your type of hardware and operating system. It is possible to reinstall the software if necessary.

3. You may call Jossey-Bass/Pfeiffer Customer Service at (800) 956-7739 between the hours of 8 A.M. and 5 P.M. Pacific Time, and ask for Technical Support. It is also possible to contact Technical Support by e-mail at *techsupport@JosseyBass.com*.

Please have the following information available:

- Type of computer and operating system

- Version of Windows or Mac OS being used

- Any error messages displayed

Complete description of the problem.

(It is best if you are sitting at your computer when making the call.)

How to Use the PowerPlugs Demos

3D Titles I and II Demos

Grab your PowerPoint audience's attention with customizable 3D title animations. 60+ animated 3D title effects (with corresponding intro music).

System Requirements

- Pentium compatible processor
- Microsoft Windows 95/98/NT/ME/2000
- Microsoft PowerPoint 97/2000/2002
- DirectX 5.0 or higher (for Windows 95)—Download DirectX for free from Microsoft
- Minimum RAM: 32 MB (48 MB when running Win NT/2000)
- Available space on hard disk: 30 MB

How to Install PowerPlugs: 3D Titles. In the PowerPlugs: 3D Titles folder, there is a file called 3DTitles-I & II-v166-Demo-Setup.exe. Double click on this file. 3DTitles-I & II-v166-Demo-Setup.exe will install the 3D Titles files onto your local hard drive. It also will automatically install it into PowerPoint.

Charts Demo

The world's most powerful PowerPoint plug-in for presenting data in dramatic charts and graphs. 100+ 2D and 3D chart templates and customization tools.

System Requirements

- Microsoft Windows 95/98/ME/NT/2000
- Microsoft PowerPoint 97/2000/2002
- Minimum RAM: 32 MB (48 MB recommended)
- Available space on hard disk: 50 MB

How to Install PowerPlugs: Charts. In the PowerPlugs: Charts folder, there is a file called Charts -v11-Demo-Setup.exe. Double click on this file. Charts -v11-Demo-Setup.exe will install the Charts files onto your local hard drive. It also will automatically install it into PowerPoint.

Headings I and II Demo Presentations.

Give your PowerPoint presentations a professional look with over 2000+ artistic slide headings and coordinated backdrops.

System Requirements

- Microsoft PowerPoint 97/2000/XP
- Microsoft Windows 95/98/NT/ME/00
- Available space on hard disk: 135 MB

How to View PowerPlugs: Headings Demo Presentations. In the PowerPlugs: Headings folder, there are two files called Headings Presentation I.pps and Headings Presentation II.pps. Double click on these file to play the PowerPoint Demo presentation.

PhotoActive FX I and II Demos

Focus your PowerPoint audience's attention on your key visuals with "one-click" photo animation. 300+ beautiful still and animated photo effects.

System Requirements

- Microsoft Windows 95/98/ME/NT/2000
- Microsoft PowerPoint 97/2000/2002
- Minimum RAM: 32 MB (48 MB recommended)
- Available space on hard disk: 50 MB

How to Install PowerPlugs: PhotoActive FX I and II Demos. In the PowerPlugs: PhotoActive FX folder, there are two files called pfx-II-v132-demo-Setup.exe and pfx-I-v132-demo-Setup.exe. Double click on theses file to install PhotoActive FX I and II demo software. It also will automatically install it into PowerPoint.

Quotations Lite Edition

This lite edition of PowerPlugs: Quotations (called *PowerPlugs: Quotations LE*) contains the fully functional database software and a selection of 250 quotations from the complete edition. Once you see the quality, power, and simplicity of PowerPlugs: Quotations for yourself, we know you'll love the full version that includes over 45,000 quotations even more. Try it today!

System Requirements

- Microsoft PowerPoint and/or Word 97/2000/2002
- Microsoft Windows 95/98/NT/ME/2000
- Available space on hard disk: 40 MB

How to Install PowerPlugs: Quotations. In the PowerPlugs: Quotations folder, there is a file called Quotations Demo setup.exe. Double click on this file. Quotations Demo setup.exe will install 250 usable quotes onto your local hard drive. It also will automatically install it into PowerPoint and Word.

Slides That Win! Demo Presentation

PowerPlugs: Slides That Win! is an electronic tutorial for business presenters with hundreds of tips and ideas on delivering successful presentations.

System Requirements

- Microsoft PowerPoint 97/2000/2002
- Microsoft Windows 95/98/NT/ME/2000

How to Install PowerPlugs: Slides That Win! Demo Presentation. In the PowerPlugs: Slides That Win! folder, there is a file called demo.html. Double click on this file. Demo.html will play the PowerPlugs: Slides That Win! demo.

SuperShapes I and II Demos

Direct your audience's attention to your key points with over 250+ customizable, animated clipart, arrows, buttons, banners and more for Power-Point.

System Requirements

- Microsoft Windows 95/98/ME/NT/2000
- Microsoft PowerPoint 97/2000/2002
- Minimum RAM: 32 MB (64 MB recommended)
- Available space on hard disk: 70 MB (100 MB for both volumes)

How to Install PowerPlugs: SuperShapes.   In the PowerPlugs: Super-Shapes folder, there are two files called ssh-II-v102-Demo-Setup.exe and ssh-I-v102-Demo-Setup.exe. Double click on one of these files will install the SuperShapes I or II software onto your local hard drive. It also will automatically install it into PowerPoint.

Templates LE

Enhance your PowerPoint presentations with the world's biggest and best collection of templates for Microsoft PowerPoint! With over 60,000 templates and backgrounds, you will always find the perfect look for that special presentations. PowerPlugs: Templates LE includes 10 world-class PowerPoint templates containing 20 stunning backgrounds in all—a welcome addition to the handful of basic templates that are included with PowerPoint.

System Requirements

- Microsoft PowerPoint 97/2000/2002

- Microsoft Windows 95/98/NT/ME/2000

- Available space on hard disk: 800 MB to install each CD

How to Install PowerPlugs: Templates LE.   In the PowerPlugs: Templates folder, there is a file called Templates Demo v10 Setup.exe. Double click on this file. Templates Demo v10 Setup.exe will install 10 PowerPoint templates onto your local hard drive. It also will automatically install it into PowerPoint.

Transitions I and II Demos

Keep your PowerPoint audience's attention with television-style 3D transition effects. 140 + TV-style 3D slide transitions effects (with synchronized sound effects)

System Requirements

- Microsoft Windows 95/98/ME/NT/2000/Office XP

- Microsoft PowerPoint 97 or 2000

- DirectX 5.0 or higher (for Win 95/98)—Download DirectX for free from Microsoft

- Minimum RAM: 32 MB (48 MB recommended when running under Win NT 4.0)

- Available space on hard disk: 6.5 MB

System Recommendations

A fast PC or—even better—a 3D graphics acceleration chip or board with 4 MB or more of video RAM. This is not required, but is very useful for speeding up the effects creation process.

How to install PowerPlugs: Transitions. In the PowerPlugs: Transitions folder, there is a file called Transitions-I & II-v166-Demo-Setup.exe . Double click on this file. Transitions-I & II-v166-Demo-Setup.exe will install the Transitions files onto your local hard drive. It also will automatically install it into PowerPoint.

6451